God's Holy Love

For Newcomers to Christian Faith

God's Holy Love

For Newcomers to Christian Faith

Martin Bleby

MARBLE MEDIA

2018

First published by
New Creation Publications Inc., Australia in 2000, 2001
Reprinted 2007

Third Edition published by Marble Media 2018

© Martin E. Bleby, 2000, 2001, 2018

National Library of Australia
cataloguing-in-publication data

Bleby, Martin E. (Martin Edward).
God's holy love: for newcomers to Christian faith

ISBN 978-0-9925376-2-3 paperback
978-0-9925376-3-0 e-book

1. God—Worship and love—Biblical teaching.
2. Christian life. I Title.

231.042

Artwork: *Martin Bleby*
Cover design: *Nicole Dunkley*

Marble Media
3 Shannon Crescent Coromandel Valley SA 5051 Australia
martin.bleby@gmail.com

Printed by CreateSpace and Kindle Direct Publishing

CONTENTS

God the Father Almighty

Weeks 1–9

Jesus Christ, His Only Son, Our Lord

Weeks 10–18

The Work of the Holy Spirit

Weeks 19–27

The Church and the Kingdom of God

Weeks 28–36

INTRODUCTION

God's Holy Love

Twice in his First Letter, John the apostle makes the astounding statement, 'God is **love**' (1 John 4:8, 16). Before that, however, comes the even more far-reaching statement, 'God is **light**' (1 John 1:5).

'Light' here is contrasted with the darkness of sin and unrighteousness, from which we need forgiveness and cleansing (see 1 John 1:6–9). So 'light' designates God's holiness and strong moral beauty and purity. 'Love' here is God's giving of His all, holding nothing back: the sending of His Son in human flesh to be the one in whom all sin and unrighteousness is fully and finally dealt with and disposed of in the action of the cross (1 John 4:9–10), to bring us into direct and intimate relationship with God and with each other (1 John 1:3, 7; 4:12).

In God, and in all God says and does, light and love—moral holiness and relational intimacy—are never apart. Some would like to have one without the other: either tolerant 'love' without moral responsibility, or moral rectitude that cares little for relational closeness. Both of these tyrannise, demean and enfeeble the human spirit. Only God Himself, by His true and faithful actions of holy love in Christ, can bring us, in freedom, to that strength and beauty of character and living that befits those made to be in His image. To set forth those actions of God, in a way that encourages our full participation in them, is the purpose of this book.

For Newcomers to Christian Faith

It has been found most helpful, for those newly come to faith in God through Jesus Christ, to introduce them early to 'the whole counsel of God'—the wise and loving plan and purpose of God as consistently set forth in the whole of the Scriptures. This Paul the apostle did, daily, for over two years, with his new converts in Ephesus (see Acts chs 19 and 20). Many great teachers of the church have done this over nearly two thousand years. In this way believers are given a reliable framework in which to understand what has happened to them, and where God is taking them in their lives.

God's Holy Love is a selection of daily readings from the Bible, with comments, carefully compiled to give new believers just such an overview of God's nature and ways, as we grow in them together. The outline is based on **The Apostles' Creed**: an early Christian summary of the teaching given by the apostles of Jesus Christ in the first century AD, which is used as a personal profession of faith at baptism. It tells us the most important things we need to believe from the Bible. It says where we stand with regard to God, life, the universe and everything. It tells us what we need to know if we are to share the message and experience of God's holy love with others.

John Calvin, in his famous *Institutes of the Christian Religion*, (published in progressively revised editions between 1536 and 1559) similarly adopted 'the arrangement of the Apostles' Creed, as that with which all Christians are most familiar. For as the Creed consists of four parts, the first relating to God the Father, the second to the Son, the third to the Holy Spirit, and the fourth to the Church, so the author, in fulfilment of his task, divides his Institutes into four parts, corresponding to those of the Creed' (John Calvin, *Institutes of the Christian Religion*, tr. Henry Beveridge, Wm. B. Eerdmans Publishing Company, Grand Rapids, 1983, p. 27).

The readings and comments are arranged for daily use, on six days a week, for thirty-six weeks. Taken over four nine-week terms, with holiday breaks in between, it can extend to a whole year's course of study.

Participants will need to have their own copy of the Bible to work from. Those new to Bible reading will need to get used to looking up the passages, perhaps with the help of an index. The Bible is made up of a number of different books in the one volume. In the references that are given each day, the title of the book is given first, followed by the chapter number, then, after the colon, the verse numbers. For instance, on Week 1, Day 1, '1 Corinthians 8:5–6' means you look up the First Letter of Paul to the Corinthians, find chapter 8, and read verses 5 and 6. On Week 2, Day 4, 'Revelation 21:9 – 22:5' means that you read in the Book of the Revelation to John (the last book in the Bible), from the beginning of verse 9 in chapter 21 to the end of verse 5 in chapter 22.

Together with Others

The daily Bible readings can be done by individuals on their own. Questions and thoughts for personal reflection are included in the text.

Provision is also made for number of people to use the book as a group. After working through the readings on their own during the week, they could come together to share experiences and insights, to address questions and issues that have arisen from the materials studied, and to give each other encouragement, advice and support for living and growing in the knowledge and love of God together. Questions and issues for group discussion are included in the text at the end of each week's readings and comments. Opportunity is given for the group to pray together.

An earlier edition of this book included an Appendix on 'Using *God's Holy Love* as Catechesis', to show how the book might be used in churches that have adopted a catechumenal process to induct and nurture new believers. While it may have been helpful in some settings (for which it is available in a separate booklet), this Appendix is no longer included. The effectual working of the word of God through the Spirit does not need to be made reliant upon any organisational apparatus. It is our hope that those who are brought to read the Scriptures, alone or in company with others, may find themselves directly in a dynamic experience of Christ.

Some who use the book as a study course may find it helpful to focus more intently on some of the material by doing written assignments: say, one each term. Possible questions for written assignments are included at the end of the book, along with a reading list.

A Personal Note from the Writer

This book is the fruit of nearly thirty years of pastoral ministry in country, outback and metropolitan South Australia. In 1993, I felt strongly constrained to gather together all that I had taught in my ministry thus far and put it in this form. This was the culmination of a process that had been going on over many years, and has continued since then. This material has been used in a number of different settings:

in home groups, as lectures, in preparation for baptism and confirmation, and for reaffirmation of faith, for personal study, and in recorded form as daily devotional material for radio or private use. It has been revised and up-dated for this publication.

I write from an Anglican background, as will be evident to any who are familiar with that stream of Christian faith and living. In that, I have sought to be faithful to the Scriptures as a whole, and to draw on what is common to the whole Christian tradition.

Among my many teachers, I pay tribute to two in particular: my father, John Bleby, who first introduced me to these wonderful realities through his preaching and teaching, in his extensive confirmation classes (carefully prepared and tirelessly revised and kept up to date), and in our family life; and my friend and colleague Geoffrey Bingham, who has opened to me the depths of the cross of Christ, as the central key to seeing and understanding the whole counsel of God.

I am grateful also to the New Creation Teaching Ministry team members, helpers and supporters, who have made this publication possible.

I give thanks to God, who has called me to know Him in this way, that I might make Him known to others; and I pray that what is set out here may help to bring many to the knowledge and love of this Holy One who has loved us with an everlasting love.

Martin Bleby
Coromandel East

In the Year of our Lord 2001

THE APOSTLES' CREED

I believe in God, the Father almighty,
    creator of heaven and earth.

I believe in Jesus Christ, God's only Son, our Lord,
    who was conceived by the Holy Spirit,
    born of the virgin Mary,
    suffered under Pontius Pilate,
    was crucified, died, and was buried;
    he descended to the dead.
    On the third day he rose from the dead;
    he ascended into heaven,
    and is seated at the right hand of the Father;
    from there he will come to judge
    the living and the dead.

I believe in the Holy Spirit,
    the holy catholic Church,
    the communion of saints,
    the forgiveness of sins,
    the resurrection of the body,
    and the life everlasting. Amen.

(Text from: The Anglican Church of Australia, *A Prayer Book for Australia*, E. J. Dwyer Pty Ltd, Alexandria, 1995, p. 12.)

GOD THE FATHER ALMIGHTY

Weeks 1–9

Week 1

CREATOR AND PROVIDER OF ALL

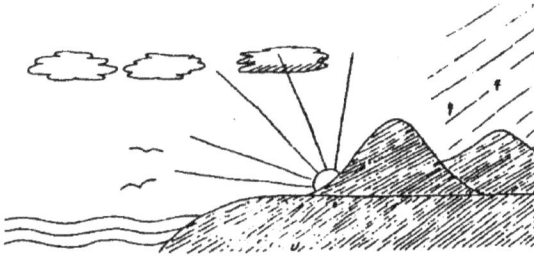

Day 1: 1 Corinthians 8:5–6

In the midst of many pressures in our lives, and the many so-called 'gods' and 'lords' that people set store by, or that seek to rule our lives, we need to know and love the true God, from whom we have come, for whom we exist.

This story is told of St Patrick (about AD 460) spreading the Christian gospel in Ireland:

> The two daughters of King Leoghain, Ethne the Fair and Fedelon the Ruddy, went early to the well to wash. There they found Patrick and his monks, and asked him who they were, and where they came from? Patrick answered, 'It would be better for you to believe in God than to enquire about our race.' The elder girl asked, 'Who is your God and where is he?' Patrick replied: 'Our God is the God of all things, the God of heaven and earth and sea and river. He dwells in heaven and earth and sea and all that are therein. He inspires all things; he quickens all things; he kindles the light of the sun, and the light of the

moon. He has a Son, co-eternal with himself, and like him. And the Holy Spirit breathes in them. Father, Son and Holy Spirit are not divided. I desire to unite you to the Son of the heavenly King, for you are daughters of a king of the earth.'

The princesses asked more questions, and were baptised. (Brother Kenneth, CGA, *Every Man's Book of Saints*, Mowbray, London and Oxford, 1981, p. 33.)

To think about: Peter the apostle says, 'Always be prepared to make a defence to anyone who calls you to account for the hope that is in you' (1 Peter 3:15). What is my faith? Where would I start from in sharing my faith with another?

Day 2: Genesis 1:1–25

Question: How does God go about creating? What does He have to work with, and what does He use to do it? What is the role of the Spirit, and of God's spoken word, in creation?

To think about: Paul the apostle says, 'Ever since the creation of the world, God's invisible nature, namely, his eternal power and deity, has been clearly perceived in the things that have been made' (Romans 1:20). What part of creation do I relate to most closely? Where in creation have I specially seen the power of God?

What difference does it make to see created things as a direct gift to me from God?

Day 3: Genesis 1:26 – 2:3

In what way are we as human beings 'in the image of God'? It must mean that we have a relational affinity with God. We are not God, but we relate with Him in a way that fits. In this context particularly, we rule over the rest of creation, as God rules over all. Often a statue or 'image' of a king was placed in a province over which he ruled to represent the king's rule in that place (in our capital city there are many statues of former sovereigns). But we are God's image, not as an immobile statue, but in a vital, living way.

Also there is a plurality, unity and interrelatedness in our being male and female (v. 27) which reflects an 'us-ness' in God (v. 26). Is this a hint of what we later come to know of God as Trinity?

The creational mandate (v. 28) covers virtually every aspect of daily human living and working. Could 'fill the earth and subdue it' mean even more: to extend the benefits of Eden (Genesis 2, see Week 6) to the ends of the earth?

Note God's full provision for everything He has made. Is anything needful lacking in all that God has made?

To think about: It has been said that human beings have been made in the image of God, so that the Son, who himself is 'the image of the invisible God' (Colossians 1:15), could become one of us, and we could participate in his sonship. What does that tell us about what it means to be 'only human'?

In what ways do I fulfil the creational mandate (v. 28) in my daily life and work?

Day 4: Psalm 104

God did not set everything going like a clock and then sit back. The Bible speaks of His constant providence (providing) and sustaining of all He has made. He is actively present to each atom and molecule, keeping it in being by His love, so it can function properly in the way it is designed. There is 'one God and Father of us all' who is not only 'above all' but also 'through all and in all' (Ephesians 4:6). Note especially verses 27–30, and the role of the Spirit (or 'breath') of God in that.

To think about: Do I prefer to think of God as remote, or 'closer than breathing, nearer than hands and feet', intimately engaged in every aspect of my life?

Day 5: Isaiah 40:12–31

This sets out, on the one hand, the foolishness and peril of attempting to ignore God, or trying some other substitute for the one true God. On the other hand, it sets out the strength and wonder of gladly being with Him.

See how God relates to the passing of the ages and the coming and going of nations as a pianist might relate to the keys on a piano—they are all set out before Him as in the present, and He plays His music across them all.

To think about: Do I say, 'My way is hid from the LORD, and my right is disregarded by my God' (v. 27)? Is this true, or does God know and care about my every move?

Day 6: Revelation 4:8–11

This is part of a vision of God. God is to be worshipped for His creation of all things. Especially as He has not created without purpose, but will faithfully bring all things to the goal He has planned. 'For from him and through him and to him are all things. To him be glory for ever. Amen' (Romans 11:36).

To think about: Peter says, 'Therefore let those who suffer according to God's will do right and entrust their souls to a faithful Creator' (1 Peter 4:19). Often we are taken through things that we do not understand at the time. Does it make a difference to know God as a 'faithful Creator', who is bringing us to the goal He has planned for us and all that He has made?

For Group Discussion:
Let each person tell of an experience of God's creation that has been significant for them, in which perhaps they have sensed the power of God (Genesis 1; Romans 1:20).

Read the 'creational mandate' (Genesis 1:28). This is the way we are structured to operate, whether we realise it or not. Find out the occupation of each person in the group, and see how it relates to the creational mandate.

Some may have instances to share of God's provision in their lives (Psalm 104).

Share insights and address questions any may have arising from the week's readings.

Prayer: *Read Revelation 4:11.*

Week 2

WHAT ARE WE MADE FOR?

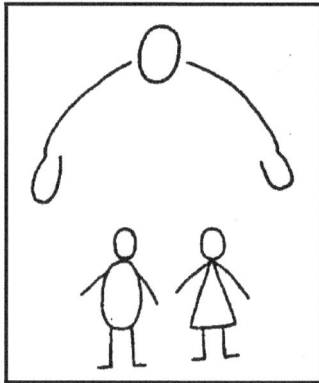

Day 1: Acts 17:24–28

The purpose for which we are made is a wholly *relational* one. Verse 27 sets it out: that we should seek God, feel after Him and find Him. Verse 28 calls us God's 'offspring'; that is, we are to relate to Him as children to the Father.

Yet verses 24–25 repudiate all human-made religion. How, then, are we to relate to God? It must all come *gift-wise* from Him—as indeed the whole of life itself does.

Note that this is not just personal and individualistic—God is working with *whole nations* (ethnic groupings) across the whole of history to accomplish this purpose of love (v. 26).

To think about: How did life come to me (or how did I come to life)? Before I was born, what had I done to apply for, or deserve, the gift of life (the gift of my self)?

'He made from one every nation of people' (v. 26). What are the implications of this for our relationships with each other: personally, racially, internationally?

Questions: Do I have a heart that seeks after God? Do I know God as the One in whom 'we live and move and have our being'? Do I *love* God?

Day 2: Ephesians 1:3–14

Verses 4 and 5 expand upon the purpose of God's will in making us. We are to be *a family of His children* ('sons' in v. 5 includes both male and female). We are to be children that match Him in holiness and blamelessness. All of this is from love, and for love, that is, intimate relationship in God. It will bring glory and praise to God: it will set forth His true nature as love (v. 6). Note that God Himself will accomplish all of this (see vv. 11–14).

This is all done 'in Christ' (v. 3. See also 'in him', v. 4; 'through Jesus Christ', v. 5; 'in the Beloved', v. 6; 'in Christ', v. 9; 'in him', v. 10). Our sonship of God is to be delineated by the one true Son, and is not apart from him. We are to be brought to participate in the relationship that the Son has with the Father! In this the Holy Spirit is active (v. 13).

Thus the whole life of the Trinity—Father, Son and Holy Spirit—is opened out to us, and we are brought right into it!

Questions: In verses 4–5: When did God choose us? What did He choose us for? What is our destination?

To think about: Read and ponder verses 1–4 of the song 'God Is Love':

1. God is love! The Father is love and the Son is the   Son of
        His love,
    The Son in this true love wants only to do all that pleases
        the Father above,
    The Spirit of love from the Father above pours out all of
        this love in the Son—
    So the Father, the Son and the Spirit all love and together in
        love they are one,
    Yes, the Father, the Son and the Spirit all love and
            together in love they are one.

2. God is love! A river of fire that can never be quenched or
        run dry,
    A love full and free that for eternity could not be just kept
        up on high:
    The Father, the Son and the Spirit all love and together in
        love they are one,
    And the love was spilled over to make all creation so others
        could join in the fun—
    Yes, the love was spilled over to make all creation so others
        could join in the fun!

3. God is love! Now look at that love in the earth and the sky
        and the sea!
    All of God's creatures in wondrous profusion all being
        what they're meant to be:
    The plants and the animals, fish and the birds, and the
        wonderful woman and man.
    All in order and harmony, working in love to partake in
        God's glorious plan!
    Yes, in order and harmony, working in love to partake in
        God's glorious plan.

4. God is love! And in that great love which God had before
   all things began,
   The Father of love with the Spirit and Son set out on this
   glorious plan:
   To make a new Heavens and Earth and a Family full of the
   fire of His love
   Where the children of God in the Spirit and Son would be
   one with the Father above.
   Yes, the children of God in the Spirit and Son would be one
   with the Father above
   (Martin Bleby, New Creation Hymn Book,
   NCPI, Blackwood, 2010, no. 281).

Day 3: Revelation 21:1–8

On any journey it is good to know where we are going, what
our *destination* is. The two final chapters in the Bible tell us
what the whole of human life and history is heading towards.

This is not just a vague and shadowy icing on the cake, but
the sure and solid goal of God's great plan. 'According to his
promise we wait for *new heavens and a new earth* in which
righteousness dwells' (2 Peter 3:13).

This is not a rubbing-out to start again with something
better. This new creation was God's plan before He set out on
His initial act of creation. It was never intended that mere
flesh and blood should inherit the kingdom of God
(1 Corinthians 15:50). If God has 'called us to his own glory
and excellence', so that we are to 'become partakers of the
divine nature' according to 'his precious and very great
promises' (2 Peter 1:3–4), then we will need not only to be
freed from all defilement and corruption but also to be
glorified and eternalised.

Note that the hallmark of this new creation is *intimate relationship with God,* as Father with son, in His immediate presence (vv. 3, 7), and the exclusion of all that does not fit with that (v. 8).

Note also that all of this happens by the initiative and action of God: the Bride/holy city (us) comes down 'out of heaven *from God*' (v. 2).

To think about: How do I anticipate the life of the age to come?

Day 4: Revelation 21:9 – 22:5

The continuation of the previous reading highlights the beauty, glory, richness and purity of us, the Bride. Verse 16 says this city is 2,400 kilometres square, and the same in height. It has room for lots of people! And they all stream in (vv. 24–26)—again not just as individuals but as nations!

Verse 22: If we are the temple of God (see 1 Corinthians 3:16)—but there is no temple in the city, but the Lord God Almighty and the Lamb is the temple—what does that say about how closely we are identified with the Father and the Son in their relationship with each other?

Questions: What are the activities of the redeemed servants of God in the holy city (22:3–5)? What needs to happen to us if nothing unclean or accursed shall enter it (21:27; 22:3)?

To think about: Jesus said to his Father, 'This is eternal life, that they know you, the only true God, and Jesus Christ whom you have sent' (John 17:3). This is not something that has to wait until after we die. Has eternal life already begun for me?

Day 5: Deuteronomy 7:6–11

This is about why God chose Israel in the Old Testament as His people. It was not through any merit or commendability on Israel's part, but purely on the basis of God's purpose of love. The same applies to His choice of us today.

To think about: What is the effect on us of 'biting the hand that feeds us', hating the One who loves us and gives us life? (see v. 10).

Day 6: Jeremiah 9:23–24

Wisdom, strength and riches are the things by which we set great store in this life. But these things do not constitute life itself. True life is knowing God as He really is. To know Him is to love Him. To love Him is to be made like Him—in 'steadfast love, justice, and righteousness in the earth'.

To think about: Do I understand and know God as He really is, or would I prefer Him to be some other way that I think would suit me better?

Question: What does Ecclesiastes 12:13 mean when it says (literally), 'Fear God, and keep his commandments; for this is the whole of being human'?

For Group Discussion:
What difference does it make to have a purpose in life? Think of times when you have had a purpose in life, and times when you have not. Share your experiences.

How much does our 'purpose in life' have to do with things, and how much with relationships?

'I know, O LORD, that the way of man is not in himself, that it is not in man who walks to direct his steps' (RSV); 'I know, O LORD, that the way of human beings is not in their control, that mortals as they walk cannot direct their steps' (NRSV, Jeremiah 10:23). How do we feel about having our purpose in life set from outside ourselves? What difference does it make to know that our purpose in life is set by God?

Rehearse the elements of God's purpose for our lives, in where He is taking us.

Share other insights and address questions that any may have from the week's readings.

Prayer: *Read 1 Chronicles 29:10–13.*

Week 3

WHAT GOD REQUIRES OF US

Day 1: Leviticus 19:1–4, 9–18

'Holy' is what God is. To be holy is to be pure and good and strong like God. We tend to have a weak, wishy-washy, 'holier-than-thou', 'so-heavenly-minded-but-no-earthly-use' view of holiness. Perhaps some quotes from P. T. Forsyth (1848–1921) can help to put us right:

> . . . by holiness is not meant anything so abstract or subjective as mystical absorption, but the whole concrete righteousness of existence, self-sustained at white heat. For our God is a consuming fire.
>
> Do let us take the holiness of God centrally and seriously, not as an attribute isolated and magnified, but as God's very essence and nature, changeless and inexorable. The holiness of God is a deeper revelation in the cross than His love; for it is what gives His love divine value.
>
> Even a loving God is really God not because He loves, but because He has power to subdue all things to the holiness of His love, and even sin itself to His love as redeeming grace (*The Cruciality of*

the Cross, NCPI, Blackwood, 1984, pp. 159, 205, 60).

To be holy as God is holy is to be with God in the burning purity of His strong love. This has some very practical outcomes (see vv. 3–18). It is, of course, totally opposed to all forms of evil.

We have seen that God's plan, which He is carrying out, is for us to be 'holy and blameless before him' (Ephesians 1:4, see Week 2). 'You shall be holy; for I the LORD your God am holy' is both a promise for the future, and a command in the present. It is made possible for us as sinners by His action of total forgiveness and cleansing in the cross.

To think about: Holiness of life begins with belonging to God. Paul, in 1 Corinthians 6:11, says, 'you were washed, you were sanctified [made holy], you were justified in the name of the Lord Jesus Christ and in the Spirit of our God'. Is holiness something I am striving for? Or is it something I already have, that I can simply live in?

Day 2: Matthew 5:43–48

This is the climax of Jesus' 'Sermon on the Mount' (Matthew 5 – 7). Jesus comes to the same conclusion as Leviticus 19:2. 'Perfect' here is not moral perfection (whatever that may be) but *relational*. The context shows that our *love* is to be as deep and wide-ranging as our heavenly Father's love—especially when it is opposed. (Perhaps this is what moral perfection is anyway, since '*love* is the fulfilling [*or* fullness] of the law', Romans 13:10).

To think about:

> Wide, wide as the ocean, high as the heavens above,
> Deep, deep as the deepest sea is my Saviour's love,
> I, though so unworthy, still am a child of his care,
> For his Word teaches me that his love reaches me everywhere.
> (C. Austin Miles, *Sing to Jesus*, Lutheran Publishing House,
> Adelaide, 1986, no. 19.)

What limits have I placed on my love? What are its cut-out points? Do I know God's love for me?

Day 3: Exodus 19:1–8

Exodus 19 gives the setting in which the ten commandments (Exodus 20:1–17) were given to Israel by God.

The important thing to realise is that they are given to people whom *God has already saved* by His love and brought to belong to Himself (vv. 4–6).

So the commandments are not something we keep so we can get God to love us and approve of us. If we belong to God by faith, we have that love and approval already. We are to keep them because *He has already set His heart in love upon us*, and we belong to Him.

If this was true of Israel, whom God saved from Egypt, how much more true is it of us whom God has rescued from sin? 'A new heart I will give you, and a new spirit I will put within you; I will take out of your flesh the heart of stone and give you a heart of flesh.' This is all done for us who are in Christ. 'And I will put my spirit within you, and cause you to walk in my statutes and be careful to observe my ordinances' (Ezekiel 36:26–27). If we are trying to keep the commandments without first receiving God's salvation and being in His love, we are missing the point entirely.

To think about: Am I trying to keep the commandments without first being saved by God? Am I even trying in that way to earn His favour and approval? If I am not accepting God's love in the way He offers it, am I really keeping His commandments at all?

Day 4: Exodus 19:9–25

This is the build-up to God's giving of the ten commandments on Mount Sinai. Is it there just to impress the people? Or to scare them into keeping the commandments? Or is it something more than that?

'Moses brought the people out of the camp to *meet God*' (v. 17). The commandments never came to us on their own. *God Himself comes with them.* In the commandments, God is revealing Himself as He really is in direct relationship with us. The commandments are *the outshining of God's own nature.*

Verse 15 enjoins a period of sexual abstinence before coming to meet God. Is this because God disapproves of sex? (How could He, since He invented it!) Or is He saying that there is something more important and lasting coming up?

Verses 12–13, 21–24: See how God is concerned to protect sinners when they meet with Him, so they are not destroyed.

To think about: Am I trying to have the commandments without God? Would I like to have God without His commandments? How do I feel about meeting God as He really is in direct relationship to me?

Day 5: Deuteronomy 4:1–14

It is God's commandments, particularly the ten commandments (v. 13), that mark off God's people from all other peoples, as those who have God with us, answering our prayer and speaking to us His word, powerful to save (vv. 6–8).

The commandments are not directives delivered from on high while God Himself remains aloof. They come with us being *gathered into His presence* (v. 10). They are never apart from a direct relationship with God. Indeed, that is what the commandments are all about: loving God with all that we are (see Deuteronomy 6:4–5) and having His life come out through us. They are *life lived in the direct presence and power of God.*

The commandments are thus the true way of life. They are given to us *that we may live* (v. 1) and that life may work properly for us. Patterned on the nature of the Creator Himself, they set forth for us *the functional operations of the universe.*

To think about: How do I hold fast to the Lord in all things day by day (v. 4)? How does it show in our lives that God is with us (vv. 6–8)? How are we passing on the commandments to our children (vv. 9–10; see also Deuteronomy 6:6–9)?

Day 6: Deuteronomy 10:12 – 11:1

God made us, and knows us, and loves us, and gives us these commandments *for our good* (vv. 12–13). To be with God in love and obedience is to do ourselves, and everyone else, the greatest favour possible!

To be with God in His love is to be *like Him* in the way we live (e.g. vv. 18–19).

To think about: What does the Lord require of me?

For Group Discussion:
Look at the various understandings of the commandments given above:

* *the outshining of God's own nature,*

* *life lived in the direct presence and power of God,*

* *the functional operations of the universe.*

How do these differ from the ways we have understood the commandments of God?

The commandments 'are never apart from a direct relationship with God'. In what ways do people try to use the commandments either (a) to get closer to God, or (b) to keep God at arm's length? (Think of examples from your own experience.)

Can we have a true morality apart from relationship with God? What would it be based on?

How possible is it to have a true relationship with God as He really is, in a way that seeks to bypass His commandments?

When God says, 'You shall be holy, for I the LORD *your God am holy', what does that mean for us? Where does it start from, and how does it work out in practice?*

Prayer: *Psalm 73:21–28.*

Week 4

OUR DUTY TOWARDS GOD

Day 1: Deuteronomy 6:1–9

Verses 4 and 5 spell out the heart of our 'duty' towards God—the relationship of total love. It starts with God being *one*. God is one in Himself—Father, Son and Holy Spirit—and His oneness is the oneness of *love-in-action*. He loves us totally with all His heart and soul and might. He works to bring our love up to the level of His own.

To think about: God's love is total. Our love is partial, or not at all. Coming into God's love is a gift—we find ourselves in the love of God. How do we know we are in the total love of God? How do we know when we are not?

Day 2: Deuteronomy 5:1–7

Verses 6 and 7 are the first commandment. We are to have no other gods but the One who has saved us out of bondage (slavery). For Israel it was slavery in Egypt; for us it is the slavery of sin and guilt. Can any other god rescue us from that? There is indeed no other true and living God. To operate truly as human beings, according to the way things actually are, we need to relate to Him alone as God.

To think about: Our 'god' is whatever we look to for satisfaction and fulfilment in life. How can we identify other 'gods' in our own lives? In the life of our community?

Day 3: Exodus 20:4–6

The second commandment forbids idolatry—the worship of anything made by God or human beings, as if that thing or creature or person itself were God. Idolatry makes no sense, for anything that is made cannot ever be God who made all things. Nor can a static object ever represent properly the dynamic, active, purposeful, loving God. Jesus said that the Father seeks us to 'worship him in spirit and in truth' (John 4:24), that is, as He really is, by the life that comes from Him.

We are made for worship, and if we will not worship (give proper worth to) God, then we must worship something else. Psalms 115 and 135 say of idols: 'those who make them *are like them*, so are all who trust in them'. For example, worship money and you will become cold and hard like money. Worship your work, and it will take over the whole of your life. The idols exercise a terrible tyranny over us. God knows that, and the harm they will do to His creatures, and so in His love He will not let us keep worshipping them. Hatred of Him will last no longer than three or four generations before people turn back to Him, yet at any point those who turn to love Him will know His mercy for ever.

To think about: Would God really love us if He was not 'jealous' for our love—if He couldn't care less whether we related with Him in love or not?

Day 4: Exodus 20:7

The third commandment is about honouring God's name. God is not a force, He is personal. He has a name. He is not a thing to be used, manipulated or pushed around. He operates in the freedom of His own being. He does His will. We who call on His name and bear His name (i.e. belong to Him) are to live fully and consistently with all of that—not in an empty way.

Read Ezekiel 36:16–28 to see how those who bear God's name can defile His reputation by their unholy living, and what God does with us to restore the honour of His name.

To think about: Jesus called God 'Holy Father' (see John 17:11). How would it show in our lives that we belong to One with that name? (See Colossians 3:12–17 for a few indications.)

Day 5: Exodus 20:8–11

The fourth commandment sets aside one day in every seven for worship, rest and recreation, and gives the other six days to work. God made our bodies and He knows what they need to function properly (Napoleon tried the 'metric week', but it didn't work!). Jesus said the sabbath was made for the benefit of humanity (Mark 2:27). It is a wonderful, refreshing gift from God.

It is also rooted in God's own being and action. God Himself is not ceaseless, restless activity. As in the act of creation, He has a plan, a purpose, a goal. When He reaches that goal, He is satisfied with what He has done, and is happy to rest in these works of His love. We should also be happy to rest with Him in trust. We must not think that our ceaseless, frenetic activity will achieve anything more than He has done.

To think about: Am I prepared to stop? Or do I think that what I am doing is too important to lay aside for a day? How does that show up where I stand with regard to trusting in God?

Am I prepared to put in a good day's work on the other six days? Or would I prefer to take it easy all the time?

Day 6: Deuteronomy 5:12–15

This version of the fourth commandment focuses on God's *redeeming* work, and our appreciation of that.

Jesus said one sabbath day, 'My Father is working still, and I am working' (John 5:17). God had finished His work of creation, but His work of providing and sustaining was still going on, and now He was about His work of redeeming, restoring and glorifying His creation. That is why Jesus healed on the sabbath day, because that is what the Father is doing now.

Israel was to remember how God had rescued them from slavery, and to give their workers and animals a rest from their labours as God had given to them.

To think about: How do I not only give myself a rest, but also make it possible for others to take a rest, one day in every seven, to the glory of God?

This is how **our duty towards God** is summarised in the Anglican Catechism (*An Australian Prayer Book*, Anglican Information Office Press, Sydney, 1978, p. 544):

> My duty towards God is,
> to believe in him, to fear him, and to love him, with all my heart, with all my mind, with all my soul, and with all my strength;
> to worship him, to give him thanks, to put my whole trust in him, to pray to him;
> to honour his holy name and his word;
> and to serve him truly all the days of my life.

For Group Discussion:

It is probably inappropriate that God's commandments should be up for discussion! We are not in a position to modify any of them—only to keep them, or not. It would be good to encourage and help one another in the keeping of them—always remembering that this can be done only in direct relationship with God, as the One who has already saved us to Himself.

Share first of all how each of these four commandments speaks to us of the truth of the way God is:

(1)   God's one-and-only-ness,

(2)   The living God as worthy of our whole worship,

(3)   God's personal freedom, and our belonging to Him,

(4) God's inner peace and rest and satisfaction, and how He brings us to share in that.

Share practical experiences, and personal difficulties, in the keeping of each of these commandments.

Prayer: *1 Chronicles 29:14–18.*

Week 5

OUR DUTY TOWARDS
OUR NEIGHBOUR

Day 1: Exodus 20:12

The fifth commandment speaks of honouring our parents. It is described as 'the first commandment with a promise' (Ephesians 6:2)—life will be longer and healthier, less stressful and more at peace if we do this than if we don't.

Parent–child relationships are the most basic in society. When these break down, society breaks up (see 2 Timothy 3:1–5. Note v. 2). Restoring these is the first step in the restoration of all things (Malachi 4:5–6).

These are patterned on the very nature of God. John 5:17–20 sets out the true relationship within the Godhead of the Father and the Son: the Son joining with the Father in all that the Father is doing, the Father counting the Son in on His every action. All fatherhood–motherhood, all family relationships, derive from God (Ephesians 3:15). Our fathers and mothers are living, solid signs among us of His fathering of us. Life flows richly as we live with each other consistently with the way He is.

To think about: What does John 5:17–20 teach me about my relationships with my parents, or with my children? See also Ephesians 6:1–4, Colossians 3:20–21.

Day 2: Exodus 20:13

Why are we to do no murder? For our self-preservation in society? (This would be a very selfish reason.) Because there is something intrinsically wrong in killing? (But then why would God in the Bible command the deaths of so many people and animals for various causes?)

God is the One who gives life, and the One who takes it away (see Deuteronomy 32:39). To murder someone wilfully (including suicide, abortion and 'euthanasia') is to interfere with that gift, and to usurp that right. It is to play God to that person, when we are not God.

Genesis 9:1–6 gives the rationale behind it. A human being is in God's image—to murder is to strike a blow against God Himself, to dethrone God and put yourself in His place, to 'kill the Author of life' (Acts 3:15). And, since He is the One from whom all our life comes, this is to strike a deathblow also against ourselves.

Jesus equated murder with *hatred*, the opposite to love. This is at the root of all murder, and is the way of death (Matthew 5:21–26; 26:52; 1 John 3:14–15, 16). On the cross this hatred and preference for death met with all the love and life of God, and was defeated.

To think about: 'Let all bitterness and wrath and anger and clamour and slander be put away from you, with all malice, and be kind to one another, tenderhearted, forgiving one another as God in Christ forgave you' (Ephesians 4:31–32).

Day 3: Exodus 20:14

Adultery is unfaithfulness in relation to marriage. ('Fornication' is a sexual relationship outside of any marriage bond; 'adultery' is a sexual relationship that intrudes on an already existing marriage. Both are included here.) It not only causes hurt and complication at the human level, but it is also a forgetting of the covenant of our God (Proverbs 2:16–17). We are made in God's image and bound to Him in covenant. God is utterly faithful to us in that. Unfaithfulness is not part of His nature. To be unfaithful in relation to marriage is to go against the way things really are.

Just as our unfaithfulness to God does not break His covenant with us, so adultery does not break the marriage bond (see Hosea 1–3; Isaiah 54:5–10; Jeremiah 31:31–34). Jesus and the early church considered that a husband and wife were bound to each other as long as they both were alive, whether separation or divorce had taken place or not, and any other marriage-type relationship entered into during that time to be against this commandment of God (see Mark 10:1–12; 1 Corinthians 7:10–11, 39). Thus marriage is patterned on God's faithfulness to us in Christ (see Ephesians 5:21–33), as a gift of His love.

Question: How does this seventh commandment show us the glory and greatness of God? What does Matthew 5:28 tell us about where adultery comes from?

Day 4: Exodus 20:15

Read also Ephesians 4:28, which says what happens when a thief turns to Christ.

Question: What does that tell us about the nature of God, in whose image we are made?

God does not have to steal glory from anyone else. He has all the riches of glory and grace. He *gives* to all His creation. He fully equips us with all we need. Receive from Him and we shall never have to steal. Rather, like Him, we shall have plenty to give (see 2 Corinthians 9:8).

Day 5: Exodus 20:16

Read also Ephesians 4:25, 29.

Question: Why are we not to lie to one another?

God is true, and the truth is God in all His actions of holy love. All things and all people hold together in Him, and belong together in truth.

Why should we ever want to make out that things are different from the way they really are? God is and lives and speaks the truth always in utter consistency. In His image, in His creation, we are to do accordingly ourselves.

Day 6: Exodus 20:17

To covet is to set your heart on something that belongs to another. This is equivalent to idolatry (Colossians 3:5; Ephesians 5:5).

God is all-sufficient, and everything is His. He gives to all who call upon Him according to their true needs. This gives us deep satisfaction in our hearts, and we rejoice with God to see what He has given others. We are content (see 1 Timothy 6:6–10).

Question: What do I covet most?

This is how the Anglican Catechism summarises **our duty towards our neighbour** (from *An Australian Prayer Book*, p. 544):

My duty towards my neighbour is,
to love [my neighbour] as myself, and to do to others whatever
    I wish they would do to me;
to love, honour, and care for my parents; to honour and obey the
    Queen and all who are in authority under her; to submit myself
    to my teachers and spiritual pastors; to be respectful and
    courteous to all;
to hurt no one by word or deed; to bear no malice or hatred in my
    heart;
to keep my body in temperance, soberness and chastity; to be true and
just in all my dealings;
to keep my hands from pilfering and stealing, and my tongue
    from evil speaking, lying, and slandering;
not to covet or desire things that belong to other people but to
    learn to work honestly for my own living, and do my duty in that
state of life to which it shall please God to call me.

The Ten Commandments Song may help you to remember the commandments in simple form:

I am the Lord your God who brought you out of the land of   slavery:
(1) Put God first, and (2) worship God only,
(3) Honour His name, and (4) keep His day,

(5) Honour your parents, (6) love, don't murder,
(7) Be pure in all you think and do and say,
(8) Don't cheat or steal, be honest and fair,
(9) Don't spread falsehood anywhere,
(10) Don't get greedy, be satisfied—
So let the Spirit of Jesus live inside!

(© Martin Bleby)

For Discussion in Groups:

Read the text which appears alongside the number of each of these last six commandments (5–10), and consider how that commandment reflects the character of God in His relationships with us:

(5)   '. . . one God and Father of us all, who is above all and through all and in all' (Ephesians 4:6),

(6)   'I kill and I make alive . . . and there is none that can deliver out of my hand' (Deuteronomy 32:39),

(7)   'A faithful God, without deceit, just and upright is he' (Deuteronomy 32:4),

(8)   '. . . ask God, who gives to all generously and ungrudgingly, and it will be given you' (James 1:5),

(9)   '. . . the King of heaven . . . all his works are truth' (Daniel 4:37),

(10)   'The earth is the LORD'S and all that is in it, the world, and those who live in it' (Psalm 24:1).

That should be enough to contemplate and revel in together, as the source and basis of all our actions!

Encourage one another in the living of these ways of God.

Prayer: *Psalm 119:33–40.*

Week 6

GOD'S GOOD RULE REJECTED

Day 1: Genesis 2:4–25

What are all the things that God provided here for the human race? Let us list them: the earth, and the heavens, the breath of life—our very being, a garden home, every tree 'pleasant to the sight and good for food', a plenteous water supply, work and responsibility, all we need to eat, guidance and limitation, all the birds and animals to be responsible for, companionship with each other, marriage and family life, in company with God (see Genesis 3:8). Is anything lacking here?

Here we have a picture of abundant provision, warm dependence, regal nobility, functional order and intimate union.

What is meant by 'the tree of the knowledge of good and evil'? Why is it forbidden to humankind? The law of God was not spelled out until much later (Exodus 20). Yet, as we have seen, if the commandments are simply the outshining of God's own nature in living relationship with us, then God's law has been in wonderful operation from the beginning (see e.g. Genesis 26:5, which is still long before Exodus 20). Here it is embodied in the 'tree of the knowledge of good and evil'. It is not for man and woman to know and decide for themselves what is right or wrong in the way that God does. That knowledge is reserved for God alone. We are to depend on and abide in Him, in this as in all things, for this is our very life.

Note: Some take this account as literal historical fact. Others see it as an instance of the Bible's use of picture language. Either way, we may learn from it the truth about God, the world, humankind, sin and redemption.

To think about: Do I *thank God* for all that has been provided? Do I *honour Him as God* in all the important issues of life (see Romans 1:21)?

Day 2: Genesis 3:1–6

In Revelation 12:9 the serpent here is identified as the Devil or Satan, a great fallen angel who had rebelled against God. 'You will not die' is one of his lies. To go against God and set our own course in this way means to die to God relationally in the immediate present—to become the living dead (see 1 Timothy 5:6; Ephesians 2:1). This later issues inevitably in physical death, since it is a rejection of the Author of life.

The root temptation here is to become 'as God' (v. 5)—to put ourselves in the place of God. This is a deep, unfounded and bitter rebellion, with no good cause or reason.

To think about: Compare verse 6 with 1 John 2:16. In what ways am I allured away from abiding in God?

Day 3: Genesis 3:7–24

Here we may list the *consequences* of this rejection of God's good rule: in our relationship with ourselves, with God, with each other, with the rest of the creation, and with the 'good life'. We have shame about the way we are, and we feel the need to cover ourselves, to hide what we are from ourselves and from other people. We also want to hide ourselves from God—our close and trusting relationship with Him is broken. We evade our responsibility for what we have done, and blame others, further damaging our relationships with each other. We are out of kilter with the natural creation, and at enmity with the evil one. Bearing children and rearing them becomes a painful exercise, and family relationships become disordered, manipulative and oppressive. The natural creation becomes antagonistic to us, work becomes a chore, and we end up in dusty death.

Yet in the middle of this are the signs of God's continuing care for the human race, and His determination to carry through His great purposes of love.

What is the hope that is held out in verse 15? It is a promise that there will be one born of woman who will deal a death-blow to the evil one, at the cost of injury to himself. How does that relate to our Lord Jesus Christ? Is not this a graphic picture of what happened on the cross?

What indications are there in this account of God's continuing care of sinners? There is the thoughtful clothing of the man and his wife to keep them warm. Even the barring of their way to the tree of life for the time being is a great mercy:

they do not have to live forever in the sin and evil they have brought upon themselves and God's creation.

Day 4: Isaiah 14:12–15

This passage, and the following one from Ezekiel, are addressed in the first instance to earthly rulers—the king of Babylon and the king of Tyre. They have also been taken to delineate the fall of angels, and of human beings, and as such are instructive commentaries on Genesis 3.

'Day Star' in verse 12 has also been translated 'Lucifer' ('Bearer of light'), another name for Satan—see also 2 Corinthians 11:14. (For a fuller picture of the fall of Satan and his angels, see Revelation 12.)

'I will make myself like the Most High' (v. 14) is the deluded ambition of Satan, and the temptation he brought to humankind. But Satan is not and never can be God, and neither are we. Such an impossible quest is brought to a fruitless doom (v. 15).

To think about: How have I ever wanted to put myself in the place of God, with regard to my own life, or anyone else's?

Day 5: Ezekiel 28:11–19

This is addressed specifically to the king of Tyre in Ezekiel's day (about 580 BC), but it is written in poetic form to read rather like the story of Adam and Eve, and it can be applied to the whole human race.

Questions: What are verses 11–15 saying about the God-given glory of a human person? (Note how the jewels in vv. 13–14 are repeated in a picture-language description of the final outcome of the human race according to God's plan of action in Revelation 21:9–21!)

Where is the 'iniquity' found (v. 15)? What form does it take (v. 17; see also v. 1)? Compare Mark 7:20–23.

Where does the 'fire' come from (v. 18)? Who brings it out? (Note: this is God speaking.) What does the 'fire' do? Compare Romans 1:28.

What does this tell us about sin and its outcome?

Day 6: Romans 3:9–18

This is a compilation of Scripture passages put together by Paul the apostle to demonstrate the desperate plight of humanity—that all are 'under the power of sin' and cannot get themselves out of it.

All would probably agree with the writer of Ecclesiastes when he says, 'Surely there is not a righteous person on earth who does good and never sins' (Ecclesiastes 7:20). But none of us can acknowledge the full and terrible extent of our sin until we know and accept what God has done in love for us to bring about our forgiveness and restoration.

To think about: 'For our sake God made Christ to *be sin* who knew no sin, so that in him we might become the righteousness of God' (2 Corinthians 5:21). What would that have meant for Christ? What does it mean for us?

For Group Discussion:

'Sin' is not an easy topic for discussion. We are all involved in it, and with it comes an inbuilt self-deception and self-justification, such that it is well-nigh impossible to get to the truth concerning sin. It can really come only by revelation and the conviction of the Holy Spirit (see John 16:8–9).

So begin by talking about the goodness of God: see Genesis 2:4–25 (Day 1). Rehearse each of the elements there, and share your experiences of them. Then talk about Romans 1:21, about honouring God as God and giving thanks to Him.

It has been said that everyone knows what is right and wrong—only we each have our own different version of it! Speak of our experiences of arrogating 'the knowledge of good and evil' to ourselves, outside of relationship with God in love and dependence, and the harm that comes from that.

What would it be like to have all your sins taken away, and all guilt removed? Romans 3:23–24: 'all have sinned and fall short of the glory of God; they are now justified by his grace as a gift, through the redemption that is in Christ Jesus'. What would that do to our attempts at self-justification?

Prayer: *Psalm 32.*

Week 7

THE WORSHIP OF OTHER 'GODS' (IDOLS)

Day 1: Romans 1:21–25

It has been said, 'The human being is a *worshipping* animal'. We have been made to worship God. But if we will not worship God, then we must turn and *worship* something else—give it that *worth* in our lives that belongs only to God. That 'something else' will not be God, but something God has made. Thus we are in a real bind: we are looking to something that is not God to give us the kind of satisfaction that only a true relationship with God can give. We will resent it when it does not come up with the goods. But by then it is too late: that idol will exercise a cold and terrible tyranny over us, and we will be locked into it. Our very thinking becomes twisted and wrong. We may think we are so brilliant, but it could be we are basing our whole lives on something that is false and mistaken. We cannot help ourselves.

To think about: Idols can be mental images as well as physical ones. What is my idol? What do I look to for my satisfaction in life?

Day 2: Jeremiah 2:9–13

God is our true glory (see Isaiah 60:19). Without God we are without glory. So we will try to get glory for ourselves in other ways. We will resort to idolatry.

Here idolatry is shown up for the shockingly unnatural thing it is. What are the 'two evils'? Why would we ever want to forsake God, and His rich provision, for the dried-up impoverishment of idols?

To think about: 'I know, O LORD, that the way of human beings is not in themselves, that it is not in us who walk to direct our steps' (Jeremiah 10:23). How much is our idolatry simply an attempt to direct our own steps, on our own terms that we have made up for ourselves?

Day 3: Isaiah 44:6–22

One of the great deceits of idolatry is that we think there could be anything that is like the incomparable God. 'To whom then will you compare me, or who is my equal? says the Holy One' (Isaiah 40:25).

Here the ridiculous foolishness of idolatry is exposed. But note in verses 21–22: Why are we to turn back to God? What idol could do what God has done, who has taken away our sins, so that we can serve Him in truth and freedom? Having idols can often be an attempt on our part to avoid a direct relationship with the living God. But why would we ever want to do that? Especially when we consider what He has done to make us belong to Himself.

To think about: What are the things we busy ourselves with most? Could it be that these are our idols? What do I allow to get in the way of my direct relationship with God in loving dependence?

Day 4: Psalm 115:3–9

This speaks of the deadening effect of idolatry—how *we become like what we worship.* Live for money, and you become cold and hard and impersonal and unfeeling, like money is. Live for your work, and it will drive you into a form of slavery. Whereas we have been made in the image of the living, loving, dynamic God, to be in all our ways like Him! Jeremiah 2:27 speaks of those 'who say to a tree, "You are my father", and to a stone, "You gave me birth"'. How could we demean ourselves to such a level of existence?

To think about: Are there times when I have nothing I am able to say, or when I am unable to listen and take things in, or to feel, or to remain otherwise than rooted to the spot? Does that tell me something about the idols I may have been worshipping—that I have become like them? How would it be different if I was relating rightly to the one true and living God?

'Not to us, O LORD, not to us, but to your name give glory, for the sake of your steadfast love and your faithfulness' (Psalm 115:1).

Day 5: 1 Corinthians 10:14–22

We know that idols are really lifeless entities, with no real existence, and that there is one true God (see 1 Corinthians 8:1–6). But there is something more sinister about idol worship than that. Wherever there is false worship, away from the one true God, then evil spirits will move in to take to themselves the worship that rightly belongs to God alone— just as Satan sought the worship of Christ himself (Matthew 4:8). Thus they will bring their adherents into terrible bondage. When Israel went in for the worship of idols, they thought it was harmless enough. But we are told, 'they sacrificed to demons, not to God'. And these evil powers drove them even to the sacrificing of their own children (see Deuteronomy 32:16–18; Psalm 106:36–38). There is a clear choice here: our worship of the one true God cannot be mixed with any worship of those rebellious powers that are totally opposed to God.

To think about: Do I seek to come to the one true God with idols of my own liking still hidden in my heart (see Ezekiel 14:1–6)?

Day 6: Psalm 63:1–4

However far we go into idol worship, we are still structured to long for God. The 'God-shaped blank' that nothing else will fill still remains inside us.

God makes His promise: 'I will sprinkle clean water upon you, and you shall be clean from all your uncleannesses, and from all your idols I will cleanse you' (Ezekiel 36:25). So we can become effective 'under-fountains' of the fountain of living waters. 'Keep your heart with all vigilance; for from it flow the springs of life' (Proverbs 4:23).

To think about: 'Little children, keep yourselves from idols' (1 John 5:21).

For Group Discussion:
Let each member of the group speak briefly on the topic: 'An idol I have known'. What would it mean in each case to 'become like what we worship'?

Focus on ways that idolatry is damaging to relationships: in marriage, in families, in the workplace, in the community, between nations or groups.

'You shall be clean from all your uncleannesses, and from all your idols I will cleanse you.' What is the connection between idolatry and the guilt of sin? How does one perpetuate the other? What needs to happen to break that vicious cycle?

Prayer: *Psalm 135.*

Week 8

WRATH—THE PRESSURE OF
GOD'S HOLY LOVE

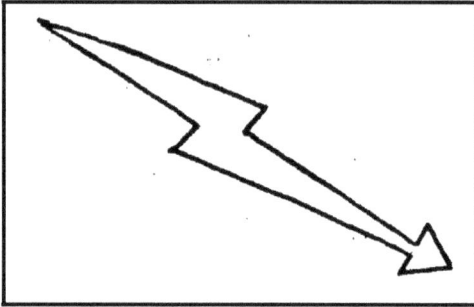

Day 1: Psalm 7:11–17

God's judgment and wrath is not a popular theme these days (I wonder why!), but the Bible bears ample testimony to it. Not just the Old Testament, but also the New (it is Hebrews 12:29 that says 'our God is a consuming fire'). God's wrath is not opposed to His love; rather, it is *the necessary action of His love against sin and sinners.* It is not automatic—it is God's personal action. He can advance it, or in His forbearance delay it, according to His purpose.

Question: If God was not opposed in wrath against evil, what kind of God would He be? Could we respect Him, or trust Him?

Can I join in Psalm 7:17? or Revelation 15:3–4?

Day 2: Genesis 6:5–22

The Genesis flood is an early example of the action of God's wrath, and a pattern of all God's judgments.

(There has been some dispute over the nature of these records, and as to whether the Flood was universal or local. Once again, we can set such controversy on one side to focus on what the text teaches us about God's dealings with humankind.)

God had made no mistake in creating everything the way it was. 'Everything he had made . . . was very good' (Genesis 1:31). So this was not a case of wanting to rub it all out and start again. This was an act of judgment against widespread evil that was doing great harm to God's good creation.

Verses 5 and 11–12 give a picture of wholesale unrestrained violence, with all vestiges of good removed. To put a stop to that was a great *mercy,* and a just *judgment.*

We are told in 1 Peter 3:20 that 'God's *patience* waited in the days of Noah, during the building of the ark'. The 'one hundred and twenty years' in Genesis 6:3 may refer to this. During this time Noah was 'a herald [or preacher] of righteousness' (2 Peter 2:5), testifying to God's coming judgment and His gracious purpose to save His faithful people, and calling the world to repentance, in the very action of building the ark (Hebrews 11:7).

The flood then comes, as predicted, in *full measure.* Note God's *grace and favour* towards Noah and his family and the animals and all their descendants.

So the flood, after due and patient warning, was a timely and merciful judgment, given in full measure, and full of grace and favour. This is the pattern of all God's actions of wrath.

To think about: How have I experienced God's judgments in my life? How have I experienced God's patient forbearance and grace?

Day 3: Romans 1:18–32

This key passage repays further close examination. It is the starting point of Paul's presentation of the gospel in this letter.

Question: How is the action of God's wrath depicted here (note especially vv. 24, 26 and 28)?

Here the action of God's wrath is to *give us up to our own (compounding) sin:* to idolatry and its ill effects, to perverted sexual relationships, and to all kinds of blatant wickedness. Note again that this is not just automatic and consequential, but the personal action of the living God. His holy love presses our sin out into the open, to leave us in no doubt as to what is really in our hearts (see Mark 7:20–23).

This has led someone to say, 'God's wrath is not sin, but sin [unconfessed, internally active] *is God's wrath*' (Geoffrey C. Bingham, *Angry Heart or Tranquil Mind?*, NCPI, Blackwood, 1991, p. 42).

This can then drive us to realise our need for God, and take up the gift of repentance (see 2 Peter 3:9).

Day 4: Psalm 38:1–22

This is a classic description of the action of God's wrath in a person's life. Note how it is seen as *God's personal action* ('your arrows . . . your hand', v. 2), driving the sufferer back to God in confession and repentance. As God has brought it on, so God is the One who will make the way out.

Question: Have I looked to God for that way out? Or am I still trying to make my own way out?

Day 5: Micah 7:18–20

One of the lovely things about God's wrath is that it comes to an end (see e.g. Isaiah 40:1–2). God is not wrath, but God is *love* (1 John 4:8, 16). God's wrath always serves the purposes of His love. God has hard words for any who keep wrath for ever (Amos 1:11), for that is not the way He is. His wrath does its job, and then ceases.

The place where God's wrath comes finally to an end is at the cross. There we see God's wrath fully and finally expended on sin, and fully borne for us and in us by God's Son. (See Mark 14:27; 15:33–34; Romans 8:3; 2 Corinthians 5:21; 1 Peter 2:24. If it is true that 'sin is God's wrath', then for Christ to bear sin and to bear God's condemnation is perhaps one and the same thing.) This is where all our sins have been cast 'into the depths of the sea'.

Question: If God 'does not retain his anger for ever', have I ever any grounds for retaining mine?

Day 6: Psalm 32:1–11

This is a wonderful prayer about how *we* come to the end of God's wrath, as a result of what He has done. What follows is a life of glad closeness to God, being led by Him in the right ways.

To think about: 'There is one whole side—the side indicated by the words, judgment, expiation, or atonement . . . which it is absolutely impossible to drop from Christianity without giving the Gospel quite away in due time. Individuals, of course, can remain Christian while they discard it, but the Church cannot' (P. T. Forsyth, *The Cruciality of the Cross*, pp. 200–1).

For Group Discussion:

'Yes, O Lord God, the Almighty, your judgments are true and just!' (Revelation 16:7). Let members of the group say how easy or how difficult each one has found it to say that in the past. How have you changed now in your understanding or acceptance of the truth of God's wrath?

Understanding and acceptance of the truth of God's wrath can come in a resentful way, or gladly. Where are we, honestly, in this regard?

Rehearse together the true elements of God's actions of wrath:

- *God's own personal action,*

- *after due and patient warning,*

- *bringing timely and merciful judgment,*

- *given in full measure,*

- *full of grace and favour,*

- *coming to an end when it has done its work.*

What have been our experiences of these elements in our lives?

How are we to understand the statement, 'God's wrath is not sin, but sin . . . is God's wrath', in the light of Romans 1:18–32?

How can a true understanding of God's wrath help us to know what was happening on the cross of Christ? How can a true understanding of what was happening on the cross help us to a right acceptance of the wrath of God?

Prayer: *Daniel 9:4–19.*

Week 9

GOD'S COVENANT FAITHFULNESS

Day 1: Exodus 34:5–9

This is a glimpse that Moses was given of God's glory (see 33:18–23). It was a spoken word by which God declared His nature.

God is a relational God. In Himself we know that He is Father, Son and Holy Spirit, in a dynamic and intimate relationship of love, as each one honours and serves and gives to and receives from the others. So God is also in determined relationship with all that He has made, and especially with His people. The expression of this relationship down through history is called God's covenant. *'Covenant' is that by which God binds Himself to His people in steadfast love and faithfulness.*

In this He is utterly true to His own holiness and righteousness, in that He will make no deal with evil or sin, but will make a way of dealing with it so He can be merciful and favourable and close to His people, and bring them to Himself.

To think about: How can God forgive iniquity and transgression and sin, but at the same time by no means clear the guilty (v. 7)? For this to be so, God would have to make some merciful and gracious provision by which the guilty would receive all that is due to them, but in a way that would then free them to enter fully into the steadfast love and faithfulness of God. If God could do that, then this would be covenant love indeed!

Day 2: Genesis 9:8–17

There is a series of covenants referred to in the Old Testament. This is the first one, with Noah and his descendants—that is, with the whole human race as it is presently constituted. It is an establishing of the covenant relationship that God has had with His whole creation from the beginning.

Part of this covenant is a staying of wrath, a holding back of further judgment (v. 11). The rainbow is taken by some as a sign that God has 'put aside his bow' (compare Psalm 7:12).

On what basis? Not on the basis of our changed behaviour—things were just as bad after the flood as before it (see e.g. Genesis 8:21; 9:20–25; 11:1–9). Only on the basis of God's own faithfulness to Himself and to us in covenant. God knew that He would be dealing righteously with sin in the full and final judgment of the cross. The final judgment upon us is withheld until then. (Some take it that the bow is set pointing at God's own heart.) Jesus is our true ark of mercy in the flood of judgment.

In the vision of God in the Book of Revelation, the rainbow is no longer just a bow. It is a full circle of light around the throne of God, declaring His covenant heart and nature (Revelation 4:3).

To think about: Have you ever thought that it is only by virtue of the cross, and the forbearance and restraining of wrath that it makes possible, that the sun still comes up each morning, the grass and trees still grow, the seasons come and go, and we are secure to live each moment of our lives (as in Matthew 5:45; Acts 14:15–17)? This is an action of God's covenant.

Day 3: Genesis 15:1–21

This is the covenant with Abraham and his descendants, that is, with the Jews, and with all who believe God as Abraham did.

Walking with another person between pieces of animals cut in half was a solemn way of making a covenant (see Jeremiah 34:17–20). It was saying, 'If I break my part of the covenant, may I be like these animals'. This is a covenant with Abraham (v. 18). But Abraham does not walk between the pieces. This is taken on for him by 'a smoking fire pot and a flaming torch' (v. 17). God Himself takes Abraham's part, as well as His own, in the forging of this covenant. Could this be the Father and the Son (see Deuteronomy 4:24, 11; John 1:18) saying, 'We will bear in ourselves the consequences of Abraham and his descendants breaking the covenant'? Is not this what happened on the cross?

Abraham was passive—he was in a deep sleep and could do nothing. His role was simply to see and believe (v. 6) and so receive the benefits of that action of God: to be counted as righteous before Him.

To think about: Faith is hearing and seeing *what God is doing* in history—past, present and future—and simply aligning yourself with Him in that.

Day 4: Exodus 24:1–11

This is the covenant with the children of Israel made with Moses at Mount Sinai.

The shedding of the blood of animals prefigures the shedding of the blood of Christ in the action that alone can bring us sinners safely to God. This is called 'the blood of the covenant' (v. 8) which binds together God and His people in righteous upholding of the law of God.

By virtue of this, the chief men of Israel can see God and eat and drink with Him and not perish (v. 11).

To think about: What does this teach us about the nature of Holy Communion, and the 'blood of the [new] covenant' (Matthew 26:28)?

Day 5: 1 Chronicles 17:1–15

This is the covenant that was made specifically with King David (about 1000 BC) and his family. It is a promise that one of his descendants will rule on his throne for ever. The New

Testament is at pains to point out that Jesus belonged to the family of David (see Matthew 1:1–17; Luke 3:23–37), and sees this prophecy fulfilled in Christ's eternal reign after his resurrection.

Once again, David is a relatively passive participant in this. His attempt to build a house for God is forestalled by God's undertaking to build an even larger 'house' for him.

To think about: Have we ever tried to build a 'house' for God—do something that would make Him indebted to us? Have we ever seen the larger 'house' that He has built for us through the ages? Can we ever outdo God?

Day 6: Jeremiah 31:31–37

This last in the series gathers up all the former covenants into the one greater new covenant that Jesus fulfilled and established for ever. It has to do with the total forgiveness of sins and with knowing God intimately with His law written on our hearts. It is even more secure than the fixed order of creation, for it comes from the heart of the God who made it all (compare Hebrews 6:13–20, commenting on Genesis 22:16–17).

Question: What is my security in life? Is it how I think or feel at a particular time? Or is it God's eternal covenant faithfulness to me in Christ?

For Group Discussion:
One of the characters in the 'Asterix' comics is ever fearful that 'the sky will fall in on his head'! Speak together of these kinds of constant, often unnamed, fears that invest our lives with discomfort, unease and

uncertainty, in the experience of ourselves or others. Where do these niggling fears come from? How are they related in any way to unresolved guilt, and the concomitant fear of judgment, that we may carry around with us?

Give examples from your own experience of how God assures us of His constant love and faithfulness. What difference does it make to the whole of our lives to be in the covenant of God?

A 'contract' is a two-sided bargain for mutual self-advantage. 'Covenant' is the way God binds Himself to us in steadfast love and faithfulness, out of the resources of His own being. What difference would it make to view our relationships in the light of 'covenant' rather than 'contract': in friendship, marriage, family relationships, business partnerships, or workplace arrangements?

Prayer: *Psalm 136 (which speaks of God's steadfast love and enduring covenant-faithfulness, as manifested both in the works of creation and providence and in God's saving acts).*

JESUS CHRIST, HIS ONLY SON, OUR LORD

Weeks 10–18

Week 10

WHO IS THE SON?

Day 1: 1 Corinthians 8:5–6

We return to this passage (see Week 1, Day 1) to examine the relationship between the Father and the Lord, Jesus Christ.

God is not God in isolation. He cannot be Father in a vacuum. He is Father of the Son. This has always been so. This is what characterises Him as Father. Likewise the Son has always been Son of the Father. This is what makes him who he is. (As we shall see also, the Spirit is the Spirit of the Father and the Son.) We are not talking about human fatherhood and sonship here, which has to do with procreation. Nor are we saying that God is *like* a human father and son. These in God are the quintessential relationships, from which all other relationships are derived (see Ephesians 3:14–15).

To think about: What does it mean that the Father is the one *from* whom are all things and *for* whom we exist, and the Son is the one *through* whom are all things and *through* whom we exist? What is the difference? Does the Father ever do anything without the Son? Does the Son ever do anything without the Father? How are we related to each?

Day 2: John 1:1–18

The Word is that by which God gives expression to all that He is and all that He does (see e.g. Genesis 1:3; Psalm 33:6; Ezekiel 3:16; Amos 3:7). It is the true expression of Himself—of all that He is. The Word is never apart from God Himself, and God never does or says anything apart from the Word. The Word is that by which God brings light (knowledge and understanding, warmth and purity) to all (see Psalm 119:105). It is by His Word that the Father makes us His children (James 1:18). The Word is indeed the true Son in the image of the Father, lacking in nothing of the Father's glory and grace. He is the one by whom we see and know God.

To think about: God is not a mere force, and His Word is not a thing. God is personal, and His Word is personal and relational.

Question: Have I received Him, and believed in His name (see v. 12)? What then am I?

Day 3: Colossians 1:11–20

'First-born' here does not refer to some time when the Son came to be. The Father and the Son have always been. 'First-born' here means the pre-eminent one. He is also the one to whom the inheritance belongs—'all things were created through him and *for* him'. This is the inheritance that he brings us into as children with him of the heavenly Father. This happens by the removal of sin through his death and resurrection. Thus he is the one who heads up all things into unity and peace with his Father and with each other.

To think about: What is the inheritance of the saints in light (v. 12)? Who has qualified us to share in it?

Day 4: Psalm 2

This psalm (often quoted in the New Testament) sets out in advance the career of the Messiah as Son of God in the midst of hostile humanity.

Those in power regard the rule of God and His anointed King as restrictive, to be resisted. But God asserts His good rule by putting His Son in place, to take up his inheritance. He is the one who brings God's anger against sin to a head. But he is also the one in whom alone the sinner is safe.

To think about: Have I come to the Son? Or am I still running from him in anger?

Day 5: Psalm 110

This psalm (also much-quoted in the New Testament) testifies to the final triumph and exaltation of the Son by the power of God, the gathering of people to Him, and his role as priest, the one in whom God and humanity are brought together.

Jesus quoted this psalm in Mark 12:35–37 to indicate that, though he belonged to the family of David, yet he is greater than David—he is the Son from God, the one from whom David himself has come (see Revelation 22:16).

To think about: 'The great throng heard him gladly' (Mark 12:37). Am I thrilled by these things, or dismayed?

Day 6: Hebrews 1:1–13

Here are gathered together all the glories of Christ in his Sonship, his inheritance, his work in creation and sustaining of all things, his imaging of the Father's glory, his saving work, his present rule, his intimacy with the Father, his righteousness and worthiness, his eternity, and his final victory in the power of the Father. What majesty! What riches! What great grace towards us!

To think about: 'This is the work of God, that you believe in him whom he has sent' (John 6:29). What God desires and requires more than anything else is that we *relate with His Son* in faith and love. Jesus said, 'Apart from me you can do *nothing*' (John 15:5).

For Group Discussion:

Examine closely Hebrews 1:1–13. Let members of the group identify what it says about:

- *the Son's relationship with the Father,*

- *the Son's inheritance,*

- *the Son's role in making and sustaining the creation,*

- *the Son's imaging of the Father's glory,*

- *the Son's saving work,*

- *the Son's present rule,*

- *the Son's intimacy with the Father,*

- *the Son's righteousness and worthiness,*

- *the Son's eternity,*

- *the Son's final victory in the power of the Father.*

Let each member of the group compose a prayer, of praise, thanks, or request, that relates one or more of these elements with his or her own experience. Share in praying these prayers together, as each is willing to do so.

Prayer: *Psalm 45:1–9.*

Week 11

WHAT IS HIS MISSION?

Day 1: Genesis 3:14–15(1);
12:1–3(2); 49:10(3)

A quick skim through Genesis shows how God's promises of the Messiah took shape in the early days:

(1) These words are spoken by God to the snake in the garden, and can be taken simply at that level. But they are also spoken to 'that ancient serpent, who is called the Devil and Satan, the deceiver of the whole world' (Revelation 12:9). The New Testament tells us, 'The reason the Son of God appeared was to destroy the works of the devil', that is, 'to take away sins' (1 John 3:4–8). He would do this as one of us, by taking the pain, guilt and consequences of our sin to death in his own body on the cross, thus finishing it for ever: 'Since therefore the children share in flesh and blood, he himself likewise

partook of the same nature, that through death he might destroy him who has the power of death, that is, the devil, and deliver all those who through fear of death were subject to lifelong bondage' (Hebrews 2:14–15).

Questions: Where is the 'serpent' damaged? Where is the 'offspring' damaged? Who comes off worse?

(2) Here the promise is made more specific: it is through a descendant of Abram (Abraham) that this blessing will come to 'all the families of the earth'.

(3) This is a prophecy of Abraham's grandson Jacob, spoken to Judah, one of his twelve sons. It is from the tribe of Judah that this one shall come who shall rule over all the peoples.

To think about: If God showed by these prophecies that He had a plan well and truly in place to deal rightly with all human sin and evil, and bring us into His blessing, can I trust Him now in the circumstances of my daily life?

Day 2: 2 Samuel 7:12–16

This reminds us of the promise God made to King David (about 1000 BC). David and his family belonged to the tribe of Judah.

At one level, this prophecy was fulfilled in David's immediate son Solomon, who built the first temple at Jerusalem, and in the kings of Judah who followed him. But David's throne was not 'established for ever' by Solomon or any of his successors, and by 500 BC there was no king left on the throne. For this kingdom to be established for ever would require one who has passed through death and rules 'by the power of an indestructible life' (Hebrews 7:16).

To think about: How would David have felt on hearing these words (see verses 18–29)? How can we feel? Can we take God at His word and pray accordingly?

Day 3: Isaiah 9:2–7

As the descendants of David ruled over Judah—some good, most not so good—the expectation arose, by the word of God through the prophets, that this promised Messiah would do what no earthly ruler could ever do: bring true peace to people's hearts, and so to the whole world, through the exercise of God's righteousness.

To think about: How do each of the titles in verse 6 fulfil the deep longings of the human heart? What is our need in life for a Wonderful Counsellor, a Mighty God, an Everlasting Father, and a Prince of Peace?

Day 4: Isaiah 11:1–9

Jesse was the father of David. This makes clear that the Messiah will arise as 'a shoot from the *stump* of Jesse'; that is, after the royal house of David has been completely chopped down. He comes right out of the roots—from that which in a sense was *before* David (see Mark 12:35–37; Revelation 22:16).

Questions: How is the Spirit of God related to the Messiah (vv. 1–3)? Who does the Messiah come for, and what are the qualities of His reign (vv. 3–5)? What is the outcome of His rule? (see picture language vv. 6–9—what does this signify?).

Day 5: Isaiah 52:13 – 53:12

This is the aspect of Messiah's rule that the disciples, the Jews of Jesus' day and ourselves find most difficult to accept. But it lies at the heart of his action of love, and was prophesied long before. It can only be received and understood by a revelation from God (53:1). This is readily forthcoming.

Questions: What is the appearance of this servant in his suffering (52:14; 53:2–3)? For whose sins is he suffering—his own or someone else's (53:4–6, 12)? How did he take it (53:7–9)? Who laid this suffering upon him (53:6, 10)? If he has 'poured out his soul to death', how can he then 'see his offspring' and 'prolong his days' (53:10–12)?

In his suffering he is scarcely recognisable as a human being, and is despised as a sinner. Yet it becomes apparent that he is suffering not on his own account but for many others, and that he is without any sin of his own. This is seen to be an action of God. He dies, and yet then he is alive to see the rewarding results of his suffering. Could there be a more apt description of what happened in Christ on his cross, and in his resurrection?

Day 6: Acts 10:34–43

Note that this is spoken by Peter for the first time to some members of the 'Gentile' (non-Jewish) nations. The blessing promised to Abraham is now beginning to come to 'all the families of the earth'.

Here Peter gathers together all that the prophets had witnessed to, as he sets out its fulfilment in their own day. Peace has been proclaimed by the Messiah 'Christ', in the power of the Holy Spirit. He has brought forgiveness of sins, and release from the power of the devil, through his deep suffering and unconquerable love and life. He rules over all and is to judge all people. Peter declares the truth and reality of this in the one he has known personally—Jesus! And it comes through to his hearers with power (see vv. 44–48).

To think about: As Peter spoke of these great events and their meaning, the Holy Spirit came and powerfully applied these things to the lives of his hearers. Has that happened to me? Do I want it to happen?

For Group Discussion:
Look again at the names given to the Son in Isaiah 9:6 (Day 3):

- *'Wonderful Counsellor': with all the wisdom of God needed to sustain true living and ruling,*

- *'Mighty God': a sovereign power outside ourselves, personally present and active among us,*

- *'Everlasting Father': giving relational security, care and discipline that is utterly trustworthy,*

- *'Prince of Peace': bringing the peace of total forgiveness, to participate in the fulfilled well-being, goodwill and favour, and untroubled harmony, that is the very life of God Himself—peace with God, peace with oneself, and peace with each other.*

Let each member of the group choose one of these, and say how it might relate to personal needs in one's own experience. How does Jesus now fulfil these roles?

Examine together the questions on Isaiah 52:13 – 53:12 (Day 5):

- *What is the appearance of this Servant in his suffering (52:14; 53:2–3)?*

- *For whose sins is he suffering—his own or someone else's (53:4–6, 12)?*

- *How did he take it (53:7–9)?*

- *Who laid this suffering upon him (53:6, 10)?*

- *If he has 'poured out his soul to death', how can he then 'see his offspring' and 'prolong his days' (53:10–12)?*

Why should such suffering be necessary on our account? What does this tell us about the love-identification of the Servant with those whose sins he has borne?

Prayer *(from the ancient Christian hymn 'Te Deum'):*

> *You, Lord Christ, are the King of glory:*
> *the eternal Son of the Father.*
> *When you took our flesh to set us free:*
> *you humbly chose the Virgin's womb.*

You overcame the sting of death:
    and opened the kingdom of heaven to all believers.
You are seated at God's right hand in glory:
    We believe that you will come to be our judge.
Come then, Lord, and help your people,
    bought with the price of your own blood:
    and bring us with your saints to glory everlasting
('English Language Liturgical Consultation, 1988', in
A Prayer Book for Australia, *p. 8).*

Week 12

BECAME ONE OF US

Day 1: Galatians 4:1–7

This passage tells us not only that Jesus is fully human, but also why he became so. It was so he could bring us into our true inheritance as children of God in intimate relationship with the Father. This was the relationship that he had always known, that he now manifested in human flesh.

The 'elemental spirits of the universe' are the lesser powers that we have subjected ourselves to through sin and idolatry (see Week 7, 1 Corinthians 10:19–20). Christ comes to break their power over us by the taking away of our guilt in the cross. In this action he removed their power to accuse us, and so freed us from their grip, so that we can belong wholly to our true Father. For this to be effective for us and in us, it must be done in our flesh, as one of us.

Question: 'See what love the Father has given us, that we should be called children of God; and that is what we are . . . Beloved, we are God's children now; what we will be has not yet been revealed. What we do know is this: when he is revealed, we will be like him, for we will see him as he is' (1 John 3:1, 2). Do we know the strength and freedom of being the children of God, or are we still in slavery to the lesser powers?

Day 2: Luke 3:23–38

Genealogies are important to us. They let us know who we are, by showing us where we belong, and who we are related to. Jesus was born into the family of Joseph, which traced its descent from King David. The genealogy in Matthew's Gospel (1:1–17) traces Jesus' forebears through David to Abraham, making the point that Jesus is there for all the Hebrew people (see Matthew 2:14–15, quoting Hosea 11:1; Exodus 4:22). Luke traces it right back to the first person 'Adam, the son of God', to show that Jesus is there for the whole human race, to restore and take us on to that sonship of God—being God's children—which we lost in Adam and Eve, in our original humanity.

Question: Do we see Jesus as being well and truly part of the human race, or do we mistakenly still see him as being in some sense outside of it? What does that mean for his relationship with us?

Day 3: Matthew 1:18–25

When we say in the creed that Jesus was 'born of the virgin Mary', we are simply relaying what we find written here and in Luke's Gospel. Those who find difficulty with this have to find ways around the clear meaning of Scripture, and a number try that in different ways. 'Science' cannot make the final pronouncement here. Science, by careful observation of repeated instances, tells us what normally happens. It cannot pass judgment on a 'one-off' incident such as this. Who knows what might happen when the Son of God becomes a human being? We can only go by what has been written here—presumably related by those most directly involved.

Whatever our interest, that is not the primary thrust of the passage. The focus is on the *action of God* through the Holy Spirit in the coming of this child, on the meaning of his name and mission—'he will *save* his people from their sins'—and on the fact that, in fulfilment of prophecy, he will be '*God with us*'.

Question: Do we see the coming of Jesus as a kind of 'Christmas fairytale', or as the direct action of God in the real world of human life and human history? Do we know him as 'God with us', the one who has saved us from our sins?

Day 4: Luke 1:26–38

Once again, the focus here is on the fulfilment of God's promise to King David, the fact that Jesus is the Son of God as promised in the Old Testament scriptures, and the irresistible action of God in bringing this to pass.

For all her open willingness before God, Mary is not a perfect or 'immaculate' person. She acknowledges her need for God as her Saviour in verse 47. There were times when Jesus himself needed to rebuke her (see Luke 2:48–50; John 2:1–5). Jesus was the Son of God before he was the son of Mary. But Jesus once said, 'Blessed are those who hear the word of God and keep it!' (Luke 11:27–28), and in that no doubt he would have included his own mother. His care for her at the time of his death is especially moving (John 19:25–27).

To think about: What amazing miracle occurred when the Holy Spirit overshadowed Mary and she conceived in her womb the holy Son of God? Jesus said, 'You must be born again . . . of the Spirit' (John 3:3–8). 'To all who received him, who believed in his name, he gave power to become children of God' (John 1:12). Is this any less a miracle?

Day 5: Luke 2:1–21

The birth of Christ is here firmly set in its historical setting. In fact it is such a turning point in history that we now date all our years from this event. (The birth of Christ is now estimated to have taken place about the years 7–4 BC. The current dating system was not devised until about AD 550, so they did pretty well for those days to get it as accurate as they did!) The birth was humble and in poor circumstances, as Jesus' later life and ministry was (see e.g. Luke 9:58), but the heavenly angels could not contain their wonder and joy.

Again, the whole gospel message is there: 'to you is born this day *in the city of David* a *Saviour*, who is *Christ* the *Lord*'.

Question: Who are those with whom God is pleased (v. 14)? They are those who have received the peace of God's forgiveness which is to be forged by Christ (see Psalm 32:1–2). Have I received this peace of forgiveness? Do I know this promised anointed Messiah as my Saviour and my Lord? Am I aware of God's favour and goodness towards me?

Day 6: Hebrews 2:6–18

This brings us back to the reason the Son of God came. This is the reason he was so fully equipped with glory and honour: 'so that by the grace of God he might taste death for every one'. To do this he needed 'to be made like his brethren in every respect' (v. 17), sin excepted (1 John 3:5).

Jesus once said of his death on the cross, 'I, when I am lifted up from the earth, will draw all people to myself' (John 12:31–33). This is the ultimate identification of love, which began with his conception and birth, but which was decided upon in the heart of God 'before the foundation of the world' (1 Peter 1:18–20).

To think about: 'The doctrine of the Incarnation [Christ coming as God in human flesh] grew upon the Church out of its experience of Atonement [being reconciled to God through the cross] . . . The divinity of Christ is what the Church was driven upon to explain the effect on it of the cross' (P. T. Forsyth, *The Cruciality of the Cross*, pp. 99, 30). Do I know that Jesus has identified with me in death, and freed me from the fear of death and judgment, and that this is nothing less than the action of God's love in me?

For Group Discussion:

Let members of the group say what Christmas has meant to each one, and what it means now. How does this relate to what we have seen here of the coming in flesh of the Son of God? How might this change our observance of Christmas?

Focus on these elements of the gospel contained in the narratives of the birth of Jesus:

- *a true human being, belonging to the race of Adam,*

- *descended from David, in keeping with God's promise of a universal ruler, who would reign for ever over all things,*

- *one who would save his people from their sins,*

- *one who would be 'God with us'.*

How would you share these elements with non-believers at Christmas time, or at any other time?

'Glory to God in the highest, and on earth peace among those with whom he is pleased!' (Luke 2:14). How can we know that we are among those with whom God is pleased? What has this got to do with 'peace', and with 'Glory to God'?

What has the coming-in-flesh of Jesus got to do with his work on the cross (see Day 6)?

Prayer: *Luke 1:46-55.*

Week 13

THE ONLY SON OF THE FATHER

Day 1: Matthew 3:13–17

This is God the Father speaking directly into our space–time universe, unable to hold back His love and good pleasure in His Son as a human being on earth. He uses words which He has spoken earlier through the prophets: 'You are my son' (Psalm 2:7), and 'my servant . . . my chosen, in whom my soul delights' (Isaiah 42:1). Jesus' baptism marks the beginning of his ministry, and prefigures its central action— going down into the waters of death with and for the sinners, and rising again to pour out the Spirit upon all God's forgiven children. This fulfils all the Father's righteousness. The Holy Spirit is right in on the act, anointing the Son for this work. The Three are One in this action of love for us.

To think about: Jesus said, 'The Father who sent me has himself borne witness to me' (John 5:37). Can I take God at His word, and accept His testimony regarding His Son, and believe in the one whom He has sent?

Day 2: John 5:2–23

All that Jesus did were the works of the Father—the actions of His Fatherly redeeming love. This healing of the paralysed man was one instance of this. In the discussion that follows, Jesus makes this clear: 'My Father is working still, and I am working'. The Father has rested from His work of creation, but His work of redemption (of saving people and bringing them, at great cost, back to Himself) and glorification (fitting them to participate in His own being and action) is proceeding in the present. The Son is intimately involved in all that the Father is doing. Jesus then lays bare the heart of their wonderful relationship: the Father loves the Son and shows Him all that He Himself is doing, the Son only does what is shown and given to him by the Father. Honour and service and giving and receiving flow freely between them. This is the true Fatherhood/Family Relationship from which all other true relationships derive, and on which they are patterned (see Ephesians 3:14–15).

To think about: Is it my desire to see all that the Father is doing, and to be with Him in His will and purpose and action? This we will find only in Christ, by God's Spirit.

Day 3: John 8:26–30

Jesus says here that the full glory of God, in which the true Father–Son relationship will be fully set forth, will be seen in the action of the cross, 'when you have lifted up the Son of man'. This is not just for us to see and marvel at, but for us to look to and be healed and participate in (see John 3:14–15; Numbers 21:4–9).

To think about: Like those bitten by the poisonous serpents, we are afflicted with the deadly poison of sin. God has given us His Son on the cross as our one cure. There he embodied and took away all our sin, and set forth the glory of his relationship with the Father. Are we going to look to him and live, or are we going to die in our sin?

Day 4: John 10:11–39

The 'good shepherd' is the true ruler of God's people, as distinct from the false rulers (see Ezekiel 34:1–31). He does not serve himself but the ones he rules over. He 'lays down his life for the sheep'. His relationship with them is patterned on the Father's relationship with the Son (vv. 14–15). As the Son lays down his life for the sheep at the Father's command, and so sets forth all of the Father's total self-giving love, he receives the Father's full endorsement and good pleasure. This is proof against all the assaults of the evil one, and finally confounds them.

To think about: 'My sheep hear my voice, and I know them, and they follow me' (v. 27). Have I heard the voice of the Shepherd, calling my name? Am I following him, or still going my own way? What does it mean to me, that he knows me?

Day 5: John 17:1–5

The relationship that has ever been between the Father and the Son is set forth fully in human flesh in the man Jesus. All that the Son has been given by the Father he has now relayed to his disciples through his teaching and his mighty works. Now he prays for the full setting out of that glory as he prepares for the agony of the cross. He knows that the only eternal life is the life that the Father, Son and Holy Spirit have in each other. He prays that his disciples, and through them all who believe, 'may be with me where I am, to behold my glory which you have given me in your love for me before the foundation of the world . . . that the love with which you have loved me may be in them, and I in them' (John 17:24, 26).

To think about: If the Father loved His Son more than He loved us, He would have held him back from the cross, and let us go. But He didn't. Any 'love' that is not total, that picks and chooses, is not love as God loves. There is a sense in which the Father's love overreached His Son to come to us. His love for us is no less than His love for His only Son. Do I know that God loves me like that?

Day 6: Matthew 11:20–30

Here Jesus displays his prayer-relationship with the Father under great duress. His ministry has failed and been rejected by his own home district (Capernaum, Bethsaida). In this Jesus sees the Father's almighty hand working His purpose of love for the lowly in heart and thanks Him profoundly. Who could know the Father in this way but the everlasting Son? How could anyone know the Son better than the almighty Father who loves him? Both delight in the power of the Holy Spirit (see Luke 10:21) in revealing the other to those who have been chosen, and so bringing us in on that relationship ourselves. Where could there be an easier 'burden' to bear?

To think about: 'Come to me, all you that are weary and are carrying heavy burdens, and I will give you rest' (v. 28). How many people, in severe and difficult circumstances, have found comfort and strength in the truth of these words! Am I one of them, or am I still hopelessly trying to carry all my burdens myself?

For Group Discussion:
Examine together the relationship denoted in these words of Jesus:

- *'The Father loves the Son and shows him all that he himself is doing',*

- *'Very truly, I tell you, the Son can do nothing on his own, but only what he sees the Father doing; for whatever the Father does, the Son does likewise',*

- *'My Father is still working, and I also am working' (John 5:20, 19, 17).*

Think about these in the light of the statement, 'This is the true Fatherhood/Family Relationship from which all other

true relationships derive, and on which they are patterned'
(see Ephesians 3:14–15, Day 2). How does this relationship
between the Father and the Son relate to the patterns of our
own experience of parenting, or being parented? How is it
beyond anything that we have known?

'When you have lifted up the Son of Man, then you will
realise that I am he, and that I do nothing on my own, but I
speak these things as the Father instructed me' (John 8:28).
How does Jesus' being 'lifted up' on the cross give full
expression to the relationship between the Father and the
Son, to open that out to others? How do we receive that
ourselves?

Prayer*: Psalm 40:1–10.*

Week 14

CRUCIFIED, DEAD AND BURIED

Day 1: Luke 18:31–34

A number of times in the latter part of his ministry in the flesh, Jesus told his disciples that he was soon to suffer and die, and rise again (see e.g. Mark 8:31; 9:31; 10:33). This was always met with (deliberate) misunderstanding and non-acceptance on the part of the disciples. But it was central to the whole thrust of Jesus' life and ministry. 'I came to cast fire upon the earth', Jesus said, 'and would that it were already kindled! I have a baptism to be baptised with; and how I am constrained until it is accomplished!' (Luke 12:49–50). This is after he had been baptised in the Jordan—Jesus was looking with great urgency towards the 'baptism' of the cross (see Mark 10:38). Jesus is clear that there is a *divine necessity* for this to happen ('the Son of man *must* suffer', Mark 8:31) in accordance with 'everything that is written . . . by the prophets'. When Peter sought to dissuade him, Jesus rebuked Peter, addressing him as 'Satan', and said, 'You are not on the side of God, but of men' (Mark 8:33). Jesus knew 'it was the will of the LORD to bruise him' (Isaiah 53:10). Peter later came to see the glory of this: 'this Jesus' he said, 'delivered up *according to the definite plan and foreknowledge of God*, you crucified and killed by the hands of lawless men' (Acts 2:23).

Question: Do I see the crucifixion as a tragic accident, or as the mighty will and purpose of God? What difference does that make to me?

> *I saw Him hanging there:*
> *I wondered why—*
> *Though He had done no wrong—*
> *He went to die.*
> *He bore all sin and won*
> *Love's victory;*
> *Then I could see that He*
> *Was there for me.*

(Martin Bleby, *New Creation Hymn Book,* NCPI, Blackwood, 2010, no. 109).

Day 2: Matthew 26:20–35

On the night he is betrayed, Jesus gives a very clear indication of what is about to happen and why. His body is going to be given up to death, his blood will be violently poured out.

This is not on his own account, but 'for you' (Luke 22:19) and for 'the many' for the forgiveness of sins, in fulfilment of the new covenant promised by God (Jeremiah 31:31–34), and with a view to the rich banquet of all God's children in the kingdom of heaven (see Isaiah 25:6–9).

Jesus reinforces this by referring the prophecy of Zechariah 13:7 to himself: 'I [God] will strike the shepherd [Christ] and the sheep of the flock will be scattered'. God will make it so that Christ stands alone in the place where the sword of God's judgment falls finally upon the sinful human race. He is there in our flesh, totally identified in love with us. He alone, the sinless one, can bear it and still stand in the Father's favour. He is there for us. We are there in him. In him we are judged, in him we are executed, and so in him we are acquitted, in him alone we live. This is our Father's love for us in the Son.

Question: Do I accept Christ's account of the meaning of his suffering, death and resurrection? What are its implications for my own life and self-understanding?

Day 3: Luke 22:39–46

Here we see Jesus entering into the deep suffering, as the sin of the world begins to impinge upon him. The 'cup' is the cup of his suffering and death (see John 18:11), the cup of God's wrath against sin (see Psalm 75:8; Jeremiah 25:15, 16, 27). It practically crushes him to death there and then in the garden: 'I am deeply grieved, even to death' (see Mark 14:33–34). Jesus knows that he must go to the cross, and prays that it will not finish him there and then in the garden: 'Let this cup pass from me'. Yet even if this is the will of the Father, he accepts this. Jesus faces what he must go through (particularly the total separation of the sinner from God that he must experience), and prays and is strengthened to carry this full will of God right through to its glorious outcome (see Hebrews 12:2; 5:7–9; 1 Corinthians 10:13).

To think about: 'Because he himself has suffered and been tempted [tested] he is able to help those who are tempted [put to the test]' (Hebrews 2:18). Do I know that 'God is faithful, and he will not let you be tempted [tested] beyond your strength, but with the temptation [testing] will also provide the way of escape, that you may be able to endure it' (1 Corinthians 10:13)?

Day 4: Mark 14:53–65

Jesus' enemies had a number of reasons for wanting to dispose of him. He had claimed to forgive sins (Mark 2:1–12, the prerogative of God), he had mixed with tax collectors and sinners (Mark 2:15–17), he had healed on the Sabbath day (Mark 3:1–6), he had shown up their hypocrisy (Mark 12:38–40), he had cleansed their temple (Mark 11:15–19), and threatened their popularity and their political security (John 11:47–53). But at the root of it all was the matter of authority (see Mark 11:27–33). If he is the Messiah, the Son of God, then they must obey him, which they did not want to do. If he is not, they must destroy him for this harmful blasphemy. Despite all evidence to the contrary, they choose this latter course.

To think about: Where do I stand, when Jesus lays his authority claim on my life?

Day 5: Luke 23:13–25

Three times Governor Pilate calls for proof of Jesus' guilt, and three times he can only say, 'I find no crime in him'. This is not enough to stop Pilate from committing his own crime in sentencing Jesus to execution. But the point has been made: Jesus is innocent. 'In him there is no sin' (1 John 3:5). If, then, Jesus has done nothing to deserve death, yet the Father sends him to it and he goes willingly, on whose account does he go?

To think about: Overheard from a tourist in the Catacomb Underground Church, Coober Pedy: 'Jesus died for His own sins—not for mine!' This spells out clearly the choice we have: Jesus either was a sinner and deserved the death he got, or else, if he was not, we are implicated ourselves.

Day 6: Luke 23:32–56

Jesus' prayer in verse 34 sets out his purpose and thrust in this whole action. He will not save himself because there is someone else more important to him than himself—us! We see this coming to early fruition in the thief on the cross alongside. Not only does the thief change to accept the justice of his own sentence, not only does he recognise in this bedraggled half-dead body hanging beside him the Messiah of God's kingdom, but also he fully expects to be admitted to this kingdom, contrary to all expectations, by virtue of what is happening for him on that cross (see 1 Corinthians 6:9–11). This is forgiveness indeed!

The mystery of the three hours' darkness, and what was happening in Jesus in that time, is something we can never plumb and, thank God, we never need to. Here the full weight of the sins of humankind blotted him out from the nearness of God. At the end of that time he cried out, 'My God, my God, why did you abandon me?' All sureness of knowing or understanding was denied him in that time. Yet that was enough to make open access to God freely available to all (v. 45—the curtain into the Holy of Holies), and the unity in loyalty and love of the Son with the Father of us all remained inviolate (v. 46). This is our salvation, our saving grace.

For Group Discussion:

Let members of the group say how their understanding of what happened on the cross has changed from how it was before, in the light of this week's readings and comments, or to indicate where they still have difficulty with what is said.

'Jesus died for his own sins, not for mine!' (see Day 5). We have a tendency to hold the events and meaning of the cross at arm's length from us, possibly to avoid its implications for us. If this young man's statement is not true, how are we implicated, both as perpetrators and as beneficiaries?

'Father, forgive them . . .' (Luke 23:34). We can find conflicting thoughts and emotions rising within us. On the one hand we may say, 'What is he trying to put on me? I haven't got anything (much) to be forgiven!' Or on the other hand we may say, 'I can't just simply be forgiven, just like that! My sin is too big and important to be put away just like that! Some special trouble needs to be taken over it!'

What does Jesus' crucifixion actually tell us about ourselves as sinners, and our need for God's forgiveness, and the cost of bringing that about?

Prayer: *Psalm 22.*

Week 15

FOR US AND FOR OUR SALVATION

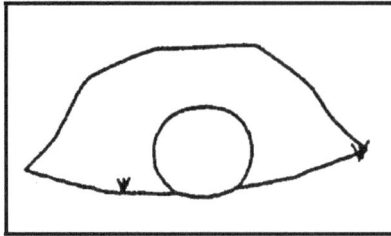

Day 1: 1 Peter 3:18–22

What happened after Jesus died? For us it is appointed 'to die once, and after that comes judgement' (Hebrews 9:27). Christ had already been through the test of judgment—and passed it. He was the one human being of whom the Father could truly say, 'You are my beloved Son, with you I am well pleased' (Luke 3:22). He did not become subject to the power of sin and death—rather, they came under his power. At the point of death he became more alive, in his spirit—no longer mortal—free and liberated as Victor and Lord. So he went into the realm of death and sin ('hell' in the original language of the Apostles' Creed means 'the place of the dead' rather than the place of final torment) and made known his victory and lordship to the disobedient spirits awaiting final judgment (perhaps those rebellious angels or sinful human beings referred to in 2 Peter 2:4, 9; and Jude 6. 'Preached' is being used here in the sense of 'announced'). If we have already accepted our judgment in the cross of Christ, we can know the same invigorating release (see John 5:24).

Be that as it may, this passage begins by telling why Jesus died. It was 'for sins'—ours, not his—to bring us to God. His resurrection declares him to be the Victor and Lord over death and all life. We come into that through baptism by our faith in him.

To think about: 'Propitiated adoption', that is, forgiveness and sonship; both 'for sins' and 'to bring us to God'—these double elements go together and constitute the whole of Christian faith and life.

Day 2: 1 Peter 2:19–25

Verse 24 must never be forgotten as central to the meaning of the cross: 'He himself bore our sins in his body on the tree [the cross]'. We know something of what it means to 'bear' our own sins—the guilt, pain, shame, dryness, confusion, defilement, the accusation—the burden of them is intolerable, and we cannot bear it. To be fully exposed to the horror of our sin would drive us mad. We know something of what it is like—all unwillingly—to bear the sins of others. That also is too much for us. Here, by one almighty act of identification in love, Christ has borne all our sin and the sin of the whole world, with all its attendant pain and shame, in his own body, and finished it there for ever. Here was pronounced and executed our final judgment as sinners. He was there for us. We were there in him.

To think about: If I hold back from this, from being one with Jesus in what he has done for me there, through faith in him, then I am on my own, stuck with my sin and destined to bear it for ever. That is hell.

Day 3: Galatians 3:10–14

Peter's reference to the 'tree' (1 Peter 2:24) may connect with verse 13 here. The best the law of God can do for those who have offended against it (all of us) is to pronounce God's curse. The law itself, and all our failed attempts to keep it, can do no more than that (v. 10). Christ, who alone has lived in all the law of God, and so is the sole inheritor of the blessing promised to Abraham, places himself, at the Father's behest, at the point where the curse is finally carried through, and bears its full force as no-one else ever could. He stands there for us, and lives to share his blessing with all who come to him by faith.

To think about: The blessings and the cursings of God's law (e.g. Deuteronomy 28) can be most disturbing for us. What is the difference when we see them all fulfilled for us in Christ?

Day 4: Romans 8:1–4

The bearing of sin, the wearing of the curse, coming under God's wrath, submitting to God's condemnation in us and for us—all is of the same piece. Paul says in 2 Corinthians 5:21: 'For our sake he [God] made him [Christ] to *be sin* who knew no sin, so that in him we might become the righteousness of God'. We cannot compute what that must have meant for

Jesus personally, let alone what it might have cost the Father, or the demands it would have made upon the blessed Holy Spirit. But it was for us, so 'for those who are in Christ Jesus' there is now '*no condemnation*'—nor can there ever be.

To think about: When Jesus said, 'It is finished' (John 19:30), he meant it. All that God had sent him to do was accomplished.

Day 5: Colossians 2:12–15

When the chief priests and officers of the temple and elders came to arrest Jesus, he said to them, 'This is your hour, and the power of darkness' (Luke 22:53). This was the time when the powers of evil were given free rein to do their worst to the Son of man. 'Many oxen have come about me; fat bulls of Bashan close me in on every side' (Psalm 22:12). This was the time when every accusation for every sin, and every vituperation of the devil opposed to God, was lodged against the human race in their holy representative. But no foothold for them could be found in the sinless Son of God, and they fell to the ground useless, expended and baffled by the power of his holy love. When all our sin is taken away, and all our guilt is purged in the cross, then the devil has nothing to accuse us of, he no longer has any hold on us and no leverage any more to prise us away from God.

To think about: 'They have conquered him [the devil] by the blood of the Lamb and by the word of their testimony, for they did not cling to life even in the face of death' (see Revelation 12:7–12). We are not to try and take on the devil in hand-to-hand combat. We could never be equal to that, for he is a powerful, devious and brilliant spiritual power. And we have something, or Someone, far better than that. If to the end of our lives we can say, 'Jesus died for me, and he has taken all my sins, and I am his, and you have no claim on me', then the devil will have nothing to accuse us of, no foothold in our lives, and no hold on us any more. ' "God opposes the proud, but gives grace to the humble." Submit yourselves therefore to God. Resist the devil, and he will flee from you' (James 4:6–7).

Day 6: Galatians 2:19–21

The whole of the cross was an action of God's love for us from beginning to end. 'When Jesus knew that his hour had come to depart out of this world to the Father, having loved his own who were in the world, he *loved them to the end*' (John 13:1). Jesus said, 'I, when I am lifted up from the earth, will draw all people to myself' (John 12:32). The identification was complete, the substitution was effected. 'The love of Christ constrains us, because we are convinced that one has died for all; therefore all have died.' We now live no longer for ourselves but for him who for our sake died and was raised (see 2 Corinthians 5:14–15). Christ's offering of himself was perfect, and effective for us all (see Hebrews 9:14; 10:10). Now we know all the love of the Father for us: 'He who did not spare his own son but gave him up for us all, will he not also give us all things with him?' (Romans 8:32).

For Group Discussion:

'*Christ . . . died for sins once for all, the righteous for the unrighteous, that he might bring us to God' (1 Peter 3:18—see Day 1). Let members of the group who know the experience of the forgiveness of sins and closeness to God share this with others.*

To bear our sins, to become a curse, to be made sin for us—these terrible things, and what they meant personally to Jesus, are beyond our computation. Nevertheless, each of us has had sufficient taste of these things in our life to know something of what they mean. Let members of the group tell of instances from their experience where such things have been borne in on them. Then try to imagine something of what it might have meant for Jesus to bear the sin of the whole world all at once.

Read out:

> *When Satan tempts me to despair,*
> *And tells me of the guilt within,*
> *Upward I look, and see Him there*
> *Who made an end of all my sin*
> *(Charitie Lees Bancroft,* New Creation Hymn Book, *vol. 1, no. 92).*

Read also Revelation 12:10–11. In the light of these, what has been your experience of both the reality of, and freedom from, accusation of sin (see Day 5)?

Looking at the passages mentioned on Day 6, trace the ways the cross of Christ brings through to us all the love of God.

Prayer: *Psalm 18:1–19.*

Week 16

HE ROSE AGAIN

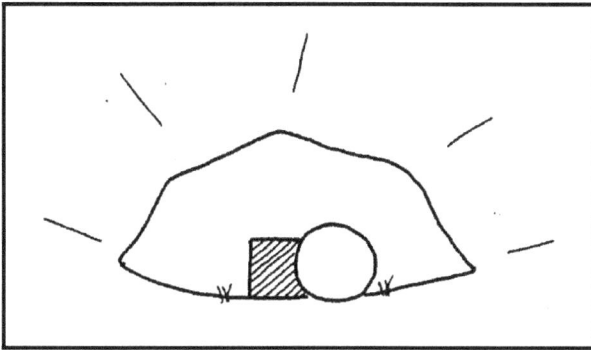

Day 1: Mark 16:1–8

It is clear that, despite Jesus' predictions of his resurrection (e.g. Mark 8:31), his disciples did not really expect him to rise again. It took a number of things to overcome their doubts and convince them. One was the empty tomb. Another was the appearance and message of the angels. But there is more happening here than just a gathering of factual information for evidence or proof. A human being has broken through the death-barrier! The death-cycle of the universe has been halted and reversed! This is a definitive action of God—a supernatural event! Hence the reaction of the women—amazement, trembling, astonishment, fear.

To think about: Nothing could ever be the same again on earth after that morning. Do I see all things in the light of the resurrection of Jesus, or do I still see them as humdrum, bounded by death?

Day 2: John 20:1–10

Here is another of the evidences—the linen grave cloths lying empty. But simply seeing the evidence, however inexplicable, is not enough. Many who have read these passages have gone to great lengths to explain them away. For Peter and the beloved disciple (John himself), as for us, there must be not only seeing but also *believing*. The evidence helps, as it did with Peter and John, the records and prophecies of the Scriptures confirm, but nothing can substitute for that warm relationship in truth and love that is *faith in God*.

To think about: Jesus said, 'If they do not hear Moses and the prophets, neither will they be convinced if someone should rise from the dead' (Luke 16:31). Can we believe in the resurrection of Jesus without 'the fear of the Lord' and the heeding of His commandments?

Day 3: Luke 24:36–43

The thing that clinched it for everyone was actually seeing Jesus risen and alive. Even so, in each recorded appearance of the risen Jesus there is reported some doubt that had to be overcome. Here Jesus convinces his disciples of the physical solidity of his resurrection body. It is the same body that was nailed to the cross and laid in the grave, which could be touched and felt and fed. Yet it is new and different: is this the 'spiritual body', referred to in 1 Corinthians 15:44? It appears to be a body free from physical limitations and completely under the control of the Lord's spirit: he can come and go as he pleases, locked doors notwithstanding. It is a real human body, freed forever from the trammels of death—as we were ever meant to be! 'Christ did truly rise again from death, and took again his body, with flesh, bones, and all things appertaining to the perfection of Man's nature' (Anglican Articles of Religion, IV, in *An Australian Prayer Book,* p. 627).

To think about: We may think it would be easier for us to believe if we had the same experience of seeing and touching the risen Jesus as these disciples had. But Luke 24:13–35 speaks of those who saw him but did not know him. Only the Scriptures and the breaking of the bread opened their eyes. We have *no less* than they had. Jesus said, 'Have you believed because you have seen me? Blessed are those who have not seen and yet believe' (John 20:29).

Day 4: 1 Corinthians 15:1–11

This is probably the earliest detailed written record that we now have of the resurrection of Jesus (written down AD 55, about twenty years after it actually happened, but referring to a form of teaching that had been around since the beginning). Note that most of those who had actually witnessed Jesus risen and alive were still there at that time to verify the facts. Some scholars claim that the different appearances reported in each of the four Gospels and here are incompatible with each other, and so are merely symbolic or even untrue. Careful work has been done to show that all the appearances are consistent and fit with each other (see John Wenham, *Easter Enigma,* The Paternoster Press, Exeter, 1984). But we should also expect that the varied accounts of such a shattering event would be multi-faceted, and still could not contain its full import.

To think about: Paul sees his own experience of the risen Christ, well after the ascension (see Acts 1:3, 9; 9:3–5), to be in direct continuity with those that happened before. Again, there is no difference for us today. Jesus had said 'I am *with you* always' (Matthew 28:20). The experience of the early church was that 'they went forth and preached everywhere, while *the Lord worked with them* and confirmed the message by the signs that attended it' (Mark 16:20). Knowing the risen Lord to be present and active in our midst remains for us the most convincing proof of all.

Question: Is this a reality for me?

Day 5: 1 Corinthians 15:12–28

We now come to the direct implications of the resurrection of Jesus for us. Apart from the fact that it designated him to be the 'Son of God in power' (Romans 1:4), and so confirmed all that he had said and fulfilled the prophecies and the promises, it assures us of two things:

(a) verse 17: the forgiveness of all our sins,

(b) verses 22–23: our own resurrection from death at the end-time.

These two belong together. For, as 'sin came into the world . . . and death through sin' (Romans 5:12), so Christ's mighty action on the cross and from the grave has won for us the victory over both sin and death. This is already fulfilled in Christ as the 'first fruits'—the initial offering as the guarantee of the whole harvest to come. Meanwhile death is still something we have to face and go through. But once death, as the 'last enemy', is destroyed, then there will be nothing holding us down, and we shall spring up to the true fullness of human life and love. This is when we shall know God our Father as our 'all in all'.

Question: When we think of the resurrection of Jesus, do we just say, 'Well, that's OK for him as the Son of God', or do we see it as the foretaste and assurance of our own resurrection? 'God raised the Lord and will also raise us up by his power' (1 Corinthians 6:14).

Day 6: Romans 6:5–11

Let us never underestimate what happened on that first Easter morning. This was no mere resuscitation. This was an unprecedented event. This was the conquest of death itself, for ever! 'Christ being raised from the dead will *never die again*; death *no longer has dominion over him*' (v. 9). With the death of death in Christ, all our enemies lie dead, and we are alive to God. Jesus truly is Lord of all.

To think about: 'If you confess with your lips that Jesus is Lord and believe in your heart that God raised him from the dead, you will be saved' (Romans 10:9).

Question: Have I ever done that? If so, what am I—saved? If I have not done that, what am I then—still not saved: still in my sins? Is there any other viable option?

For Group Discussion:

Try an exercise of heart and mind. 'When it was evening on that day, the first day of the week, and the doors of the house where the disciples had met were locked for fear of the Jews, Jesus came and stood among them and said, "Peace be with you"' (John 20:19). Take a little time to imagine that you are in that house with the disciples before Jesus came. How are you feeling? What are you thinking?

Then have someone read Luke 24:36–37: 'Jesus himself stood among them and said to them, "Peace be with you." They were startled and terrified, and thought that they were seeing a ghost.' What is going through your mind and spirit now?

Have someone read aloud the rest of Luke 24:38–43, while others listen with eyes closed. Who do you see? What is he to you? . . . 'Thomas answered him, "My Lord and my God!"' (John 20:28).

The empty tomb and grave cloths, the message of the angels, and the appearances of the risen Jesus himself, as testified to us by the apostles, help to awaken our faith. But 'knowing the risen Lord to be present and active in our midst remains for us the most convincing proof of all' (Day 4). Let members of the group speak of times when they have known the risen Lord Jesus present and active with them. Compare this with Paul's experience in 2 Timothy 4:14–18.

Prayer: *Psalm 16.*

Week 17

HE ASCENDED INTO HEAVEN

Day 1: John 20:11–18

The Gospels testify to a period of time after Jesus rose from death before he ascended into heaven. Luke in Acts 1:3 designates this as forty days—hence the period between our festivals of Easter Day and Ascension Day. During this time 'he presented himself alive after his passion by many proofs . . . speaking of the kingdom of God'. In this very personal appearance to Mary Magdalene, Jesus speaks to her of his coming ascension. 'Do not hold me' does not mean he was not to be touched. Rather it means, 'Do not try to hang on to me'—he will not always be accessible in this physical way. 'I am ascending to my Father'—for all the picture language that is used (e.g. 'He ascended into heaven, and is seated at the right hand of God the Father almighty'—Apostles' Creed), the ascension means for Jesus first of all simply being *with the Father,* in His immediate presence. However, by the action of the cross and resurrection his Father has now become *our Father*, his God is now *our God*. So there is a sense in which Jesus takes us with him, even now.

Certainly, Jesus did not cease to be human when he ascended. Someone has said, 'He loved his body so much he took it with him'! It is also true to say, 'Glorified dust is now at the right hand of God'.

Question: Do I think of Jesus now as being no longer human, but as somehow having 'gone back to being God'? What is the effect of that on my present life and relationship with him?

To think about: 'He has passed beyond our sight, not to abandon us but to be our hope, that where he is *we might also be* and reign with him in glory' (*An Australian Prayer Book*, pp. 168–9).

Day 2: Luke 24:44–53

At this point Jesus summarises what has happened, and says what is now to be, as set out in the Old Testament Scriptures. Repentance and forgiveness of sins, arising from Christ's suffering and resurrection from death, are now to be proclaimed to all the nations. This is not to be done without the Holy Spirit, the 'power from on high' promised by the Father. In the light of this, the separation of the disciples from the visible presence of Jesus is no grief to them but rather a cause of great joy (as in John 14:28; 16:7).

Question: Do I think of Jesus now removed from me and 'far above the starry height', or do I take seriously his promise, 'I am with you always, to the close of the age' (Matthew 28:20)?

Day 3: Acts 1:1–11

Luke, writer of both the Gospel and the Acts of the Apostles, says that in his Gospel he 'dealt with all that Jesus *began* to do and to teach, until the day when he was taken up'— implying that the Acts tell of what Jesus then *went on* to do and teach, *after* his ascension (see also Acts 26:16; 18:9–11; 2 Timothy 4:16–18). Again here is the promise of the Holy Spirit, and the commission to bear witness to Jesus throughout this present age, until his coming-again.

To think about: The message of turning back to God and the forgiveness of sins, the outpouring of the Holy Spirit, and the knowledge that all times and seasons are in the Father's good hands—what more do we need than this to be getting on with it?

Day 4: Philippians 2:1–11

In what does Christ's exaltation consist? Is it a mark of his power over all things? Indeed it is, but what is the nature of his power? It is something very different from brute force. It is the power of true humility in God's love. This is not something that Jesus just 'put on' for his time on earth, and then laid aside again when he ascended. This is the true expression of the nature of God which he bore, by which he poured all of himself into our humble flesh. Note that there is no word for 'though' in the original of verse 6. The whole action, from start to finish, is the consistent expression and honouring of the true humility of God. It is this that makes Jesus 'Lord' over all things, since he has shown that it is this power of love alone that will prevail. That is why Paul the apostle tells us to have the same mind among ourselves.

Question: Do I look to the ascended Jesus as a source of triumphalist power to counteract my humiliating circumstances and my own deficiencies, or do I acknowledge and exercise and rejoice in the true power of his full and humble love in my life?

Day 5: Ephesians 1:15–23

We must always remember that Christ on our behalf has gone on to all the things that still await us, and possesses them in their fullness already. Paul the apostle prays that we may see these things that are ours in him in verses 16–19. Christ rules in all these things not for himself but for us, the church (v. 22), which he is now filling with all his fullness. Hence in the next chapter Paul says that God has already 'raised us up with him, and made us sit with him in the heavenly places in Christ Jesus' (Ephesians 2:6). These things we hold now and live in by faith, as we await their full unveiling at his coming appearance.

To think about: 'If then you have been raised with Christ, seek the things that are above, where Christ is, seated at the right hand of God . . . For you have died, and your life is hid with Christ in God' (see Colossians 3:1, 3).

Day 6: Revelation 1:9–20

The elements of this vision of the risen, ascended, glorified Jesus spell out what he is doing in this age. His is all the glory, authority, purity and dynamic love of God. His word is all-sufficient and deeply satisfying. His intimate concern is for the whole church of God's beloved people, and his only weapon, powerfully effective, is the word that comes from his mouth. How fearfully wonderful, in the cut and thrust of human history, and in our daily lives, to hear him speaking to us!

To think about: Do I see the churches as that gathering of people among whom the Lord Christ is walking to affirm, warn, rebuke and encourage? Or do I think that he has left them pretty much to their own devices?

Do I love the church as much as he does?

For Group Discussion:

It is common to think of the Son of God becoming human at his 'incarnation', and then going back to being God at his ascension. It comes as a surprise to us that he is still fully human—one of us—at the right hand of God. Let members of the group say how they thought about this before, and how they see it now. What difference does this make to the way we think about Christ as the Son of God? What difference does it make to the way we think about ourselves as human beings?

Some translations of Philippians 2:6 have 'though he was

in the form of God' ... he emptied himself ... humbled himself'—as though these things were something of a come-down for one in such an exalted position. Actually the words 'though he was' are not in the original text. The meaning is rather, 'being in the form of God'—in other words, the emptying and humbling were the actual expression of what God is! What difference does this make to our notion of God's glory, and of our own? What difference does this make to the ways we are to conduct ourselves in life (see Philippians 2:1– 4)?

'God, who is rich in mercy ... raised us up with him and seated us with him in the heavenly places in Christ Jesus' (Ephesians 2:4, 6). Paul speaks of this as a present reality in our experience of God's saving grace—we are already ascended with Christ! How can this be so? What difference is it to make in our lives (see Colossians 3:1–4)?

Prayer: *Ephesians 1:16–23.*

Week 18

HE WILL COME AGAIN

Day 1: 1 Corinthians 15:20–28

This passage maps out this present age in which we live, called in the New Testament the 'last days', between Jesus' resurrection and his coming-again, the penultimate (next-to-last) age. The goal is the handing over of the kingdom of all things to God the Father, that God as Father may be known to be all in all. This present age is the time of putting down of all things that oppose God's Fathering of us. There is a fierce battle raging, and it is little wonder that in the smoke and noise we are sometimes confused. But there is no doubt as to who is in charge, and the outcome is assured.

To think about:

> In this great hour they had but one word, and it came in such unity as things on earth have never known, and that one word was the full truth of the mystery, which, if a man know, he need never know more . . . for the one word to which they gave voice in their freedom, and their self-knowledge, and their knowledge of all things was this, 'ABBA!' . . . This is a word used in some Eastern languages for 'Father' (Geoffrey C. Bingham, *Bright Bird and Shining Sails*, NCPI, Blackwood, 1981, p. 121).

Question: If this is where we are heading, am I ready for this now? 'Beloved, we are God's children now; it does not yet appear what we shall be, but we know that when he appears we shall be like him, for we shall see him as he is. And every one who thus hopes in him purifies himself as he is pure' (1 John 3:1–3).

Day 2: Luke 21:25–28

When Jesus ascended, the angels said, 'This Jesus, who was taken up from you into heaven, will come in the same way as you saw him go into heaven' (Acts 1:11). They were bearing out what Jesus had spoken much about in the days of his flesh. It is often called his 'second coming', on the basis of Hebrews 9:28: 'Christ, having been offered once to bear the sins of many, will appear a second time, not to deal with sin but to save those who are eagerly waiting for him'. While the end-time has many fearful elements, for those who know Christ it is a time of great hope and expectation. If we know him now, it will then be like welcoming an old friend. If we have refused to know him here, his coming then will be a fearsome thing for us (see Mark 8:38).

To think about: 'And now, little children, abide in him, so that when he appears we may have confidence and not shrink from him in shame at his coming' (1 John 2:28). What does it mean for me to 'abide in him'?

Day 3: Matthew 24:3–14

Many would like to know how to predict Christ's coming, and when the 'close of the age' will occur. Jesus told us there would be many false leads and deceitful claims (how many have we known in our own lifetime?). Jesus here tells us clearly that before the end comes there will be an increase in apostasy (turning away from God), error and wickedness, great tribulation for God's people, and world-wide preaching of the gospel (vv. 9–14). Even so, 'of that day or that hour *no one knows,* not even the angels in heaven, nor the Son, but only the Father. Take heed, watch; for *you do not know* when the time will come' (Mark 13:32–33).

Sometimes people write of Jesus' return as if it will be known only to a few. But Jesus himself taught otherwise: 'For as the lightning comes from the east and shines as far as the west, so will be the coming of the Son of man' (Matthew 24:27), 'and every eye shall see him' (Revelation 1:7)—it will be universal, public, observable, but an event far beyond anything we have ever experienced—the end of all things as we have known them.

To think about: Why are we so keen to know the timing and nature of Christ's coming again? Is it because we are still more concerned about our own 'kingdoms' than with the kingdom of the Father who fixes the times and seasons by His own authority? (See Acts 1:7.)

Day 4: Mark 13:9–23

In Jesus' dissertations on the coming of the end, it is virtually impossible to extricate and distinguish what he is saying about predicted contemporary events (such as the sacking of Jerusalem in AD 70) from what he says about the end itself. It seems in his own mind they are closely associated. The end is always only this far above our heads, and from time to time it breaks in on our present experiences with dynamic force. God is ruling His world! Whether in the events of this life, or in the life to come, it is good to know Him with us, speaking through us.

To think about: 'I have told you all things beforehand' (v. 23). This means that there is nothing that happens that is outside his purvey—his ordering and provision.

Day 5: Matthew 24:42–51

Knowing that there is an immediate endpoint towards which we are working, and an answerability when we get there, gives purpose and urgency to everything we do. This can be very constructive. It is only a misunderstanding of Christ's coming-again that leads us to be other-worldly or idle. Lord Shaftesbury (1801–1885), the great social reformer in Britain, achieved much of practical value that changed the lives of many people. Near the end of his life he was heard to say, 'I do not think that in the last forty years I have lived one conscious hour that was not influenced by the thought of our Lord's return'.

To think about: 'Even if the world ends tomorrow, I will still plant my tree today' (Martin Luther).

115

Day 6: 2 Peter 3:10–14

The coming of the Lord, and all that it will bring, is in fact the motive power of all ethical and holy living. 'What sort of persons ought you to be' indeed? Life is too short for anything that is wasteful or not good. And if the outcome is going to be righteousness, holiness and purity, in unity, love and peace, then let us match ourselves to that here and now! For nothing else will last into the new creation but that which is wrought in us by the Holy Spirit of God. It is in the light of his coming particularly that we are to relate with one another in the church: 'Let us consider how to stir up one another to love and good works, not neglecting to meet together, as is the habit of some, but encouraging one another, and all the more as you see the Day drawing near' (Hebrews 10:24–25).

To think about: What elements in my life still do not match with the 'new heavens and a new earth in which righteousness dwells'? How would I live differently if I knew that Jesus was coming tomorrow?

For Group Discussion:
Go through together the events delineated in 1 Corinthians 15:20–28 (see Day 1). What difference does it make for us to see this whole age in which we live, from the resurrection of Jesus to his coming-again, as 'the last days'?

'If we know him now, it will then be like welcoming an old friend' (Day 2). What things would make us glad of the coming-again of Jesus? What things would make us fearful of it?

'You do not know when the time will come' (Mark 13:33, see Day 3). What experience have you had of those who seek to predict precisely the time of Christ's coming-again? Why do we want to be able to predict it?

What about those who think Jesus will never come again, and that things will go on just as they are (see 2 Peter 3:3–9)? Why do we want things to be that way? What difference does it make to our way of life to know that Jesus could come again at any time?

Prayer: *Isaiah 64:1–5a.*
Can we join in the prayer of Revelation 22:20? (This is the second-to-last verse in the Bible):

> *The one who testifies to these things says,*
> *'Surely I am coming soon.'*
> **Amen. Come, Lord Jesus!**

THE WORK OF THE
HOLY SPIRIT

Weeks 19–27

Week 19

WHO IS THE HOLY SPIRIT?

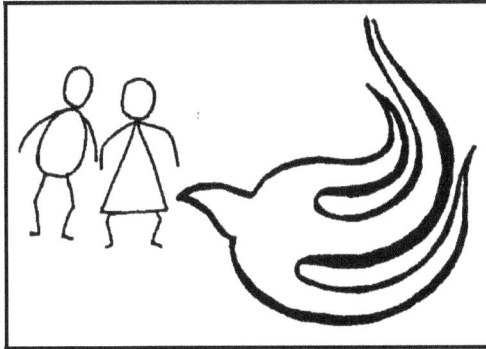

Day 1: 1 Corinthians 2:1–5

We should know by now that becoming a Christian does not mean just giving intellectual assent to certain concepts and forms of words, or even taking up certain modes of behaviour. Something happens *inside* a person—it is a matter of the heart or inner being. How does this come about?

Paul here sets no store on the form or mode or impressiveness of his presentation of the gospel, other than to say that it has to do exclusively with 'Jesus Christ and him crucified'. Paul did not resort to 'lofty words or wisdom', and he came 'in fear and in much trembling'. It is clear that people were not convinced by Paul's persuasiveness, nor by the power and confidence of his personality. Faith comes by an action of *God*, what Paul calls here 'in demonstration of the *Spirit* and of power'. Something happens inside people that they know could not have happened by any human agency. That way, people come to faith knowing that God is at work. 'Jesus Christ and him crucified' is real to them.

To think about: 'We know, brethren beloved by God, that he has chosen you; for our gospel came to you not only in word, but also in power and in the *Holy Spirit* and with full conviction' (1 Thessalonians 1:4–5). Is this how faith has come to me?

Day 2: 1 Corinthians 2:6–11

One of the psalms says, 'Out of the depths have I called to you, O LORD' (Psalm 130:1), and another replies, 'Deep calls to deep in the roar of your waters' (Psalm 42:7). It is in the depths of the human heart that God must work to purge us and bring us to Himself, and He does that by opening out to us the depths of His own heart of love and drawing us in. How can He do that but by His own Spirit, who searches the depths of God, and of all created things including ourselves, and so is able to communicate to us all the good that God has in store for us in His 'plans for welfare and not for evil, to give you a future and a hope' (Jeremiah 29:11). This wisdom of God, 'which God decreed before the ages for our glory', is denied us in this age, apart from the Spirit, and is unknown to the 'wisdom' of this world. 'The human heart and mind are very deep' (Psalm 64:6). We cannot even understand our own inner workings, or what is really needed there. Who can? 'I the LORD test the mind and search the heart' (Jeremiah 17:10).

To think about: The Spirit brings the deep things of my heart to God, and brings the will of God to bear on them: 'The Spirit helps us in our weakness; for we do not know how to pray as we ought, but that very Spirit intercedes with sighs too deep for words. And God, who searches the heart, knows what is the mind of the Spirit, because the Spirit intercedes for the saints according to the will of God' (Romans 8:26–27).

Day 3: 1 Corinthians 2:12–16

What is communicated to our hearts by the Spirit gives us an understanding of the things of God that we could never have just by living in the world. This is because in the world we have tried to live without the Spirit in a way we were never designed to be, and we have rejected the gifts of God. But now that the Spirit has broken through all that with the power of Christ and his cross (see 1 Corinthians 1:18–24), we have a completely new way of looking at things—as they really are. 'We have the mind of Christ'!

Question: Do I still try to see things according to my own 'lights', or only by the true light of the Spirit?

Day 4: Ezekiel 37:1–14

As we read this passage, it is instructive to note that the same Hebrew word 'ruach' is used for every occurrence of the English words 'breath', 'wind' and 'Spirit'. What can be more intimate with us than our own breath, the very air we breathe? So is the Spirit intimate with God—God's very life-breath. And here the whole action of giving life to God's moribund people is a work of the Spirit from God, whether as a gentle movement of air, or as a rushing, mighty wind.

To think about: The hymn, 'Breathe on me, breath of God', is a prayer to the Spirit, for a kind of mouth-to-mouth resuscitation.

Day 5: Isaiah 63:7–14

God never moves amongst His people apart from His Holy Spirit. Here God puts His Holy Spirit in the midst of His people and their leaders (see Numbers 11:16–17, 24–29). The Spirit is not a 'thing' or a 'force'. Being the Spirit of God, the Spirit is as personal as God. The Spirit can be 'grieved' by rebellion (v. 10; see also Ephesians 4:30 and 1 Thessalonians 5:19). This does not mean that the Spirit goes away. The Spirit is able to be grieved by a rebellious situation precisely because he is *still there.* That is what makes it worse. It is also the Spirit who ultimately brings us rest (v. 14).

Question: Have I received the Spirit that is from God? If so, do I ever mistakenly think then that the Spirit has left me? Or do I believe that 'the gifts and the call of God are irrevocable' (Romans 11:29)?

Day 6: John 16:13–15

Matthew 10:20 tells of 'the *Spirit of your Father* speaking through you'. Galatians 4:6 says, 'God has sent the *Spirit of his Son* into our hearts, crying "Abba! Father!"' Here we see the Spirit taking all that the Father has given to the Son, to open it out to us. Truly the Spirit is the Spirit of the *Father* and the *Son*, or indeed the 'spirit of sonship' (Romans 8:15)— of the *relationship* that is between the Father and the Son in all their rich, self-giving fullness. Two things the Spirit gets us to say are, 'Abba! Father!' (see Romans 8:14–16), and 'Jesus is Lord!' (1 Corinthians 12:3). The Spirit is very self-effacing, in that he does not draw attention to himself and will not speak on his own authority—only what he hears—and points us to the Son, and to the Father. But then, each member of the Trinity serves, honours and gives to the others, and to us, and so in this the Spirit is simply being consistent, according to God's own nature.

To pray over: What a wonderful Spirit, who brings us right into the very life of God, holding nothing back!

For Group Discussion:
Some wonder whether they have been filled with the Spirit or not. 'Two things the Spirit gets us to say are "Abba! Father!" (see Romans 8:14–16), and "Jesus is Lord!" (1 Corinthians 12:3)' (Day 6). We are told we are not able to say these things truly from the heart except by the Holy Spirit. If these things are relationally true for you, are you not already filled with the Holy Spirit of God? Let members of the group say what these two sayings or cries from the heart mean for them.

By the same token, the coming of such a one as the Spirit of God is not likely to pass unnoticed! Hebrews 6:4–5 speaks of 'those who have once been enlightened, and have tasted the heavenly gift, and have shared in the Holy Spirit, and have tasted the goodness of the word of God and the powers of the

125

age to come'. Let members of the group speak of their experiences of becoming partakers of the Holy Spirit.

These passages speak of the Spirit coming to us when we are weak and helpless, in fear and trembling, or even dry and dead. Let members of the group identify times when the Spirit has helped them in their weakness.

'The Spirit is able to be grieved by a rebellious situation precisely because he is <u>still there</u>' and has not gone away (see Day 5). Sometimes having the Spirit with you can make things worse for you for a time. There may be members of the group who have known such times, who would be willing to say how this happened, and how they came out of it.

Prayer: *Psalm 51:10–12.*

Week 20

THE SPIRIT IN THE OLD TESTAMENT

Day 1: Genesis 1:1–3

Here is the Holy Spirit, right at the beginning, actively engaged in the work of creation. The Spirit holds everything in readiness for the Word to leap out from God into the darkness, to effect the bringing of everything into being:

> We are given the image of the Spirit of God brooding over the formless deeps in which nothing exists because nothing is separated, over-shadowing them as one day he will overshadow a girl in Nazareth. The great wings of his otherness are outstretched in the primal dark and dimly reflected in the face of the waters below. Out of those depths of undifferentiated chaos all the multitudinous forms of existence are going to be beckoned into being by call and response. But in that timeless moment nothing is present except the ardent, cherishing love, the irresistible will for communion, of the Go-Between Spirit (John V. Taylor, *The Go-Between God: The Holy Spirit and the Christian Mission*, SCM Press, London, 1978, p. 26).

The Spirit is one with the Word in the Father's mighty action of creation. So Psalm 33:6 says: 'By the word of the LORD the heavens were made, and all their host by the breath [*ruach*: spirit] of his mouth'.

To think about: What difference does it make to know that the Spirit who lives in me now is the same Spirit of God that was at work in the mighty act of creation?

Day 2: Psalm 104:24–35

Here the work of God's Spirit in sustaining and renewing the whole of creation is set out (see v. 30). There is not a breath we can take or a move we can make without the Spirit of the living God. No less are the judgments that come (vv. 32, 35) actions of the Holy Spirit.

The Creator Spirit also inspires the gifts of human creativity. In Exodus 31:1–5 the Lord said to Moses, 'See, I have called by name Bezalel the son of Uri, son of Hur, of the tribe of Judah: and I have filled him with the Spirit of God, with ability and intelligence, with knowledge and all craftsmanship, to devise artistic designs, to work in gold, silver, and bronze, in cutting stones for setting, and in carving wood, for work in every craft'. Quite a range! But then we shall see that the Spirit is unstinting in the giving of gifts.

To think about:

> Where You are not, we have nought,
> Nothing good in deed or thought,
> Nothing free from taint of ill
> (Archbishop Steven Langton,
> *Veni sancte Spiritus*, circa AD 1200).

Can I say that is true of me?

Day 3: Numbers 11:16–30

One thing that the *Nicene Creed* says about the Holy Spirit is that he 'has spoken through the prophets'. True prophecy in the Bible is speaking a message that comes from God. This is never without the Holy Spirit. 'No prophecy ever came by human will, but men and women moved by the Holy Spirit spoke from God' (2 Peter 1:21). This has always been the case. 'Many years you bore with them, and warned them by your Spirit through the prophets' (Nehemiah 9:30; see also Ezekiel 2:2; Micah 3:8). 'The testimony of Jesus is the spirit of prophecy' (Revelation 19:10): all prophecy points us in one way or another to God's action in Christ (see 1 Peter 1:10–12). Here Moses longs for the Spirit of God to come upon all God's people, that all may speak God's word. The fulfilment of this begins in the New Testament at Pentecost.

To think about: Does our church run on the basis of bright ideas we have, or on the word of God brought to us by the Spirit?

Day 4: Judges 15:9–20

Where did the secret of Samson's great strength lie? Not in his long hair—that was simply a sign of his vow of dedication to God. In each instance it was because 'the Spirit of the Lord came mightily upon him' (see also e.g. Judges 13:25; 14:6). Without that, Samson was weaker than a kitten (see vv. 18–19; also 16:20, 28). The same is true of all the great men and women of God (see e.g. Numbers 27:18; Judges 3:9–10; 6:34; 11:29; 1 Samuel 10:10–11; 16:13). The same is true of us morally and spiritually, if not physically as well: without the Spirit from God, we are helpless. In the Old Testament the Spirit can come and go (see e.g. 1 Samuel 16:14). John the Baptist was told of Jesus, 'He on whom you see the Spirit descend *and remain*, this is he who baptises with the Holy Spirit' (John 1:33).

To think about: 'I know that nothing good dwells within me, that is, in my flesh. I can will what is right, but I cannot do it . . . likewise the Spirit helps us in our weakness' (Romans 7:18; 8:26).

Day 5: Isaiah 11:1–10

Here we focus upon the coming of the Spirit upon the Messiah. See also Isaiah 61:1–4. Some churches use verses 2–3 in an ancient Confirmation prayer for strengthening by the Spirit of God (see, for example, *A Prayer Book for Australia*, p. 90). This signifies our involvement by the Spirit in the mission of Christ, towards the coming of the new creation in which righteousness dwells.

To think about: How has the Spirit of God caught me up into the ministry of Christ?

Day 6: Joel 2:26–32

Here is another promise in the Old Testament that the Holy Spirit would be poured out on all people (vv. 28–29). The setting is the blessing of God and the taking away of the people's shame (vv. 26–27), and a time of terrible judgment, in which 'all who call upon the name of the LORD shall be delivered' (see vv. 30–32). So in the New Testament we find the blessing of God and the forgiveness of sins coming out of the terrible judgment of the cross to all who call upon God, through the outpouring of the Holy Spirit, at the inauguration of the era of the 'last days' (see Acts 2:1–47).

To think about: We are now in the era when the Spirit of God has flooded the earth. Have I breathed and drunk him in? Or are my mouth and nose and ears and eyes still shut tight against him?

For Group Discussion:

It would be good for members of the group to revel in their experiences of the liveliness of the Spirit of God in the whole of creation, and in creative human endeavours (see Days 1 and 2). Remembering at the same time that we live in a 'fallen' creation, as a fallen race, 'subjected to futility' (Romans 8:20), where the Spirit is engaged in exercising judgment as well as blessing (as in Psalm 104:24–35). Let members of the group identify instances of this as well. How readily do we acknowledge our total dependency upon God's Spirit for all things?

Revisit Judges 15:9–20. Trace in the narrative Samson's inability to do anything apart from the Spirit of God, and God's faithfulness to Samson in this, in keeping with His covenant-purposes, despite Samson's crassness and unworthiness.

In Isaiah 11:1–10 and 61:1–4, trace how the Spirit is given to the Messiah for the purposes of reconstituting the creation and its peoples, along the lines God had ever intended for them. How are we to participate in that action?

Prayer: *Isaiah 63:7–16.*

Week 21

THE SPIRIT AND JESUS

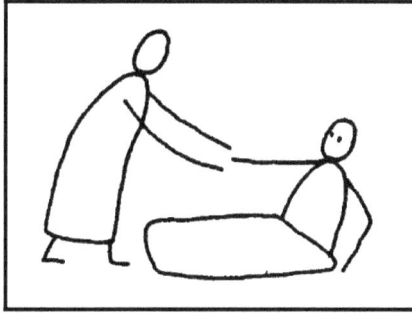

Day 1: Luke 1:30–35

As with the work of creation, so in the great work of God in redemption through Christ, nothing happens apart from the agency of the Spirit. Here Christ's very conception in the womb of Mary (so microscopic and vulnerable!) is by the mysterious and miraculous life-generating activity of the Holy Spirit of God: 'the power of the Most High will overshadow you' (v. 35)—'that which is conceived in her is of the Holy Spirit' (Matthew 1:20).

To think about: The eternal Son of God was content to be entirely in the hands of the eternal Spirit for the fragile, tiny and hazardous processes of human conception and birth— what utter trust! And the powerful, caring Spirit honoured him in that and brought him through it and beyond, according to the eternal Father's direction and purpose. Are we as willing and content to be at the mercy of the Spirit?

Day 2: Luke 3:21–22

The coming of the Spirit upon Jesus at his baptism was empowerment for his special and unique ministry as Messiah. This did not begin until the Spirit came in this way. From this empowerment flowed all that Jesus did in his ministry. Peter later put it this way: 'God anointed Jesus of Nazareth with the Holy Spirit and with power . . . he went about doing good and healing all who were oppressed by the devil, for God was with him' (Acts 10:38).

To think about: God the Father said to John the Baptist, 'He on whom you see the Spirit descend and remain, this is he who baptises with the Holy Spirit' (John 1:33). The same Spirit who empowered Jesus is the Spirit he now gives us to participate with him in his Messianic ministry.

Day 3: Luke 4:1–15

Immediately after His baptism, Jesus went into a time of testing, where he was confronted by God's antagonist the devil, who had his own self-serving purposes counter to the kingdom of the Father. But it was the Spirit who led Jesus (or 'drove him'—Mark 1:12) out there for this fierce and decisive encounter. It was the Spirit who had filled Jesus (v. 1) who now enabled and sustained him in faithfulness to the Father through all this, and it was 'in the power of the Spirit' that he returned quietly triumphant (v. 14). John 3:34–35 speaks of the Father's love for the Son, how the Father has given all things into the Son's hands. It says how the one sent from God speaks God's words, and then explains how this is so by saying of the Father: 'it is not by measure that he gives the Spirit'. This was Jesus' own constant and deeply-felt experience of the fullness of the Holy Spirit, as the gift of the Father.

To think about: When we are taken through difficult and testing times, does it help us to know that it was the Spirit himself who took Jesus into that and through it and securely out the other end, in the love and faithfulness of the Father?

Day 4: Luke 4:16–21

Right at the beginning of his ministry, in the synagogue at his own home town of Nazareth, Jesus took the Messianic prophecy of Isaiah 61 and applied it to himself. Many of us are under the misconception that Jesus did all his miracles and mighty works by virtue of some unique power he had, as God the Son, which is not available to us. Jesus in his flesh as man had no power other than the power of the Holy Spirit. 'If it is *by the Spirit of God* that I cast out demons', said Jesus, 'then the kingdom of God has come upon you' (Matthew 12:28). What he did was nothing more than could be done by any human being filled with the Spirit of God.

To think about: Jesus said, 'Very truly, I tell you, the one who believes in me *will also do the works that I do* and, in fact, *will do greater works than these*, because I am going to the Father [i.e. in the victory of the cross and resurrection, to

135

pour out the Spirit on *you*!]' (John 14:12). How does this change my understanding of the work of the Spirit in Jesus, and in me?

Day 5: Luke 10:13–22

It was the Spirit who sustained Jesus in the intimacy of his filial relationship with the Father through times of adversity in ministry (such as his rejection in the towns of Chorazin, Bethsaida and Capernaum; see vv. 13–16) and through times of rejoicing (at seeing the disciples engaged in effective ministry; vv. 17–20). In all these things he 'rejoiced in the Holy Spirit and said "I thank you, Father" '(v. 21).

To think about: If it is by the Holy Spirit that the Son rejoices in his knowledge of the Father's gracious will, and delights to carry it out, what is the role of the Spirit in our coming to know the Father and the Son (v. 22)?

Day 6: Romans 1:1–4

Christ's greatest work—the suffering and death on the cross and the rising again from the grave and the ascension into heaven—was wholly enabled from start to finish by the presence and power of the Holy Spirit. Who can plumb the depths of the mystery of what was happening on the cross—particularly between the Father and the Son ('an agony and bliss of love . . . the forsakenness and the ultimate trust'—John V. Taylor, *The Go-Between God*, p. 102)? Yet we are told that Christ 'through the *eternal Spirit* offered himself without blemish to God' (Hebrews 9:14). How was Christ able to commit his spirit to the Father (Luke 23:46) and step down into death as its conqueror, except by being 'made alive in the Spirit' (see 1 Peter 3:18–19)? Likewise the mystery of resurrection life coming into the human corpse in the darkness of the sealed tomb on Easter morning: 'vindicated in the Spirit' was how Paul put it in 1 Timothy 3:16. And here in Romans: 'designated Son of God in power according to the Spirit of holiness by his resurrection from the dead' (v. 4). No less his ascension to rule over all things was by 'the working of his great might' by that same 'immeasurable greatness of his power' (see Ephesians 1:19–23).

To think about: It is because the Holy Spirit himself has been intimately engaged in the whole work of God in Christ that he personally can now bring these 'depths of God' (1 Corinthians 2:10) and impart them to our depths. It is 'the immeasurable greatness of his power *in us who believe*' (Ephesians 1:19). It doesn't stop there, but looks towards our ultimate resurrection in glory: 'If the Spirit of him who raised Jesus from the dead dwells in you, he who raised Christ Jesus from the dead [i.e. the Father Himself] will give life to your mortal bodies also through his Spirit which dwells in you' (Romans 8:11).

For Group Discussion:

Try to imagine back to the time just after you were conceived, before you were implanted in the wall of the womb; and when you began to grow there: 'so microscopic and vulnerable! . . . the fragile, tiny and hazardous processes of human conception and birth'. Consider how Jesus was carried trustingly through all that by the Spirit of God. 'Are we as willing and content to be at the mercy of the Spirit' (see Day 1)?

Think of difficult and testing times that you have gone through, in the light of the reality that the Spirit 'drove' Jesus into the wilderness to be tested by the devil, and that he returned from there 'in the power of the Spirit' (see Day 3). Sometimes we like to think of God as rescuing us from such times, but not always of Him actually taking us into them, and seeing us right through them from beginning to end. How does this help us see them differently? Let members of the group share and reflect on such experiences.

'Very truly, I tell you, the one who believes in me will also do the works that I do and, in fact, will do greater works than these, because I am going to the Father' (John 14:12). What are these 'greater works' that we now do in the power of the Spirit from the Son? 'What he did was nothing more than could be done by any human being filled with the Spirit of God' (Day 4). How does this change the way we view Jesus, and the working of the Spirit in us?

Jesus, in the midst of great setbacks and strong encouragement in his ministry, 'rejoiced in the Holy Spirit and said "I thank you, Father"' (Luke 10:21). Consider the fullness and intimacy of this cry. How does the Spirit bring us such fullness and intimacy with the Father in the ups and downs of our lives? Let members of the group share their experiences of this, or their need for it.

Prayer: *Psalm 69:1–6, 14–18, 30, 32–36.*

Week 22

THE PROMISE OF THE SPIRIT

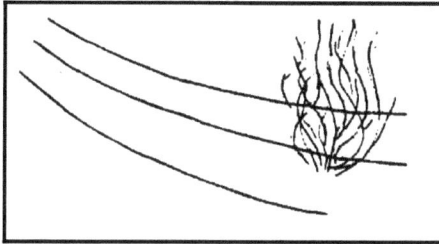

Day 1: Luke 3:15–18

John's prophecy was that the Messiah would baptise with 'Holy Spirit and with fire' (v. 16). Remember that 'spirit' can also mean 'breath' or 'wind'. A rushing, mighty wind and tongues of fire were the signs that accompanied the coming of the Spirit on the day of Pentecost (see Acts 2:1–4). Here the meaning of the signs is given, and they have to do with God's purposes of judgment and salvation. Messiah comes with the wind of the Spirit to separate the wheat from the chaff—to save the 'wheat'—and by the fire of the Spirit to burn the 'chaff'.

To think about: The Holy Spirit is sometimes called 'the Comforter'. 'Comfort' is a word that means originally strength and encouragement. Here the strong 'comfort' he brings is the assurance that God's purposes of holy good will be fully executed and carried through.

Question: What is the 'wheat' and what is the 'chaff'? (See 1 Corinthians 3:10–15 for a similar analogy.)

Day 2: John 7:37–39

Jesus makes it clear that he is the one through whom the Holy Spirit is poured out. We must come to him and 'drink'; that is, believe in him and ask. The quotation is from Proverbs 4:23: 'Keep your heart with all vigilance, for from it flow the springs of life'. We need the Holy Spirit for us to be restored to the normality and fullness of living and loving. Something must happen before the Spirit can be given—Jesus must be 'glorified'. This is a reference to the cross, and the resurrection and ascension that followed from it (see John 12:27–33; 13:31–32; 17:1–5). After that, it will be the season of the Spirit. 'As yet the Spirit had not been given' is literally, 'It was not yet Spirit', as we would say, 'It is not yet Spring'. Once the season of Spirit has begun, we need to keep our eyes and ears and nose and mouth shut tight *not* to be filled with Holy Spirit.

To pray about: Jesus said: 'If you then, who are evil, know how to give good gifts to your children, how much more will the heavenly Father give the Holy Spirit to those who ask him' (Luke 11:13).

Day 3: John 14:12–27

Here we see the Holy Spirit in full relationship with the Son and with the Father, in the movement of the love of God towards us. The whole action of the Trinity is engaged in taking up residence in us, to bring us into full participation in the operations of God's great enterprise. This is the heart of Christian experience.

To think about: In each section of this passage, trace what each 'member' of the Trinity is doing. How does that relate to the action of the other two? How does it relate to us?

Day 4: John 15:26 – 16:15

These words, and those of the preceding passage, are spoken by Jesus to his disciples on the night before he died. Up to this point he had said very little about the Holy Spirit—now he sets out the full action of the promised Holy Spirit. The previous passage was mostly about the Spirit's action towards believers. This passage refers particularly to the Spirit's ministry through believers to the world, as the gospel is brought to bear in the hearts of unbelieving sinners. As the disciples bear witness to Christ crucified and risen, the world is brought to conviction regarding:

(a) **Sin**—their refusal to believe in the one given by God who brings the forgiveness of sins,

(b) **Righteousness**—not our right action, but Jesus himself as vindicated in the work of the cross, resurrection and ascension,

(c) **Judgment**—the sentence of condemnation executed decisively by Christ in the cross and resurrection over Satan and his world-system of evil (vv. 7–11).

For this to happen, the disciples themselves must be taught by the Spirit the deep things of God (vv. 12–15). He speaks only of and from the Father and the Son in their joint love-action. Note the generosity of the Father towards the Son (v. 15). Note the Spirit's honouring of the Father (v. 13) and the Son (v. 14).

Question: Now that the Spirit has come, am I part of the Spirit's witness, or am I still part of the unbelieving world? Is there any other option?

Day 5: John 20:19–23

The first act of the risen Jesus is to bring to his failed and fearful disciples the peace of forgiveness that he has forged in the furnace of the cross. Jesus breathes his Holy Spirit on them, for them to take this experience of forgiveness to others. They carry the decisive word of the cross. This brings total forgiveness to all who receive it, and the painful burden of unforgiven sin to all who reject it. Luke's account of this same reality is in Luke 24:47, 49: 'repentance and forgiveness of sins should be preached in his name to all nations . . . I send the promise of my Father upon you; but stay in the city, until you are clothed with power from on high.'

Question: Have I received the peace of God? Am I looking to the Holy Spirit to be able to bring that peace into the lives of others?

Day 6: Acts 1:1–8

The risen Jesus refers back to the prophecy of John the Baptist (see Luke 3:16, Day 1), which is shortly to be fulfilled (v. 5). The coming of the Spirit, under the authority of the Father, will empower the disciples to witness to God's action in Christ.

Question: How often have I attempted to do something off my own bat, without waiting for 'the promise of the Father'— the empowerment of Holy Spirit?

For Group Discussion:

Why does John the Baptiser use the picture language of 'wind' and 'fire' of the Holy Spirit? What does the wind and fire do? Why should that be necessary? How does this action differ from the gentler aspects of the Spirit's 'comfort' that we may have preferred to think about before? How does this action of the Spirit relate to the action of the Cross (Days 1 and 2)? How have we known the Spirit's actions of 'wind' and 'fire' in our own lives?

Read through together John 14:12–27 (see Day 3), and together trace in each section what (i) the Father, (ii) the Son, and (iii) the Holy Spirit, is doing. Where are we in each of these actions?

In John 16:7–11 (see Day 4) look at the three areas in which the Spirit convicts the unbelieving world: sin, righteousness, and judgment. How does each of these areas relate to Jesus? Why is this so? How do we see this conviction happening in the world?

In Acts 1:4 the risen Jesus told his apostles to 'wait' for the empowerment of the Spirit before they went out to witness to

Jesus. Why should this be necessary? Let members of the group speak of times when they or their church have tried to act without 'waiting' for the Spirit, and times when they have waited for the Spirit before taking action.

Prayer: *Psalm 123. Note the stressful pressures under which this prayer is made, and the willingness to look only to God's hand before making any move.*

Week 23

THE COMING OF THE SPIRIT

Day 1: Acts 2:1–21

This was the outpouring of the Holy Spirit upon the disciples in Jerusalem (about 120 in all—see Acts 1:15). Peter saw this as the fulfilment of the prophecy of Joel (Joel 2:28–32, see Week 20, Day 6). The era/season of the Spirit has begun! The 'last days' are here! The message quickly spreads to thousands of others in Jerusalem, and they too come into the same experience (see Acts 2:37–41).

So full are they with the reality of God's wonderful action in Christ, that their hearts spill over with it and they speak it out (v. 11). On this occasion it comes out in other languages intelligible to Jews from foreign parts. The Spirit is taking the different languages that originated from man's sin as a barrier to communication (see Genesis 11:1–9), and is using them in unity and harmony to magnify God, as a sign that all the nations will bring their riches into the Kingdom of God (Revelation 21:24–26).

To think about: The effect of the coming of the Spirit at Pentecost is that we 'prophesy'; that is, we 'tell out the wonderful works of God'. Is that the effect of the Spirit in my own life?

Day 2: Acts 2:22–47

Jesus had said of the Spirit who proceeds from the Father, 'he will bear witness to me' (John 15:26). As soon as Peter is filled with the Spirit he immediately tells people about Jesus—particularly his saving death, resurrection and ascension. Peter holds nothing back in declaring the responsibility of his listeners for the death of Christ (v. 36), but makes it clear that this was 'according to the definite plan and foreknowledge of God' (v. 23), who raised him up from death 'because it was not possible for him to be held by it' (v. 24).

The effect of Peter's preaching was dynamic in bringing repentance and faith to those who heard it (vv. 37–38). Baptism to belong to Christ was the obvious outcome, with the concomitant forgiveness of sins and gift of the Holy Spirit. The life that followed from that (vv. 42–47) was rich in truth, love and power.

Question: Have I repented towards God? Have I been baptised into Jesus Christ? Are all my sins forgiven? Have I received the gift of the Holy Spirit? Am I living richly in truth, love and power?

Day 3: Acts 8:4–25

Those filled with the Spirit on the day of Pentecost were all Jews in Jerusalem. Jesus had said that it would not stop there but spread to 'Samaria and to the ends of the earth' (Acts 1:8). The Holy Spirit marked each stage of this progress with a significant initial outpouring, in the presence of the apostles of Jesus. The despised Samaritans (see 2 Kings 17:21–41; also John 4:1–42; Luke 10:25–37) were next on the list, and Peter and John were present to see it happen. An amazing unity of a new people of God was being forged by the work of Christ through the Spirit of God. Simon the magician discovered that the Spirit is sovereign, and cannot be bought or sold.

To think about: 'All who are led by the Spirit of God are sons [sons and daughters] of God' (Romans 8:14). Am I led by the Spirit of God, as God's own daughter or son, or would I prefer to do some leading myself?

Day 4: Acts 10:30–48

The Jews first, then the Samaritans, and now the Gentiles— those belonging to the nations that dwell in the uttermost parts of the earth (see Acts 1:8). Peter again is present, this time very much against his own judgment (see Acts 10:1–29), but brought here by God to be again the one who unlocks the door by which people enter the kingdom of heaven (see Matthew 16:19). The process was now in full flight. In keeping with God's promises to Israel (summarised by Paul in Romans 15:7–13), the Gentiles, along with the Jews and Samaritans, were now full participators in the people of God and of Christ (see Ephesians 1:11–14; 2:1–22). The Jewish Christians questioned this—so scandalous it seemed to them (see Acts 11:1–18)—but found that they could not withstand God.

Question: At what point did the Holy Spirit interrupt Peter's sermon? What does that tell us the Spirit is most intent on bringing through to us?

Day 5: Acts 19:1–7

The Spirit has now been poured out on all flesh—Jews, Samaritans, and Gentiles—but each person who comes to Christ must receive the Holy Spirit. Here Paul made sure that these twelve or so in Ephesus were lacking in nothing: faith in Christ, baptism, and the gift of the Holy Spirit. The effects in their lives were no different from what he had done in those who had received him earlier. This was the universal experience of believers in Christ (see Galatians 3:1–5). 'Anyone who does not have the Spirit of Christ does not belong to him', said Paul (Romans 8:9). It is as well to be sure that we do.

Question: Am I trying to belong to Jesus Christ without the Spirit which filled him?

Day 6: Romans 5:1–11

This passage reminds us again what the Spirit brings to us when he comes. 'God's love has been poured into our hearts through the Holy Spirit who has been given to us' (v. 5). What is this love the Spirit brings to us? The next verse tells us (v. 6): 'While we were still weak, at the right time Christ died for the ungodly'. Verse 8: 'God shows his love for us in that while we still were sinners Christ died for us'. And verse 10: 'While we were enemies we were reconciled to God by the death of his Son'. The Spirit applies the work of the cross in our lives. He has nothing else besides that to give us, for in giving us that, God has given His all (see Romans 8:32; John 16:15). This is all our justification, our peace, our hope, our salvation and reconciliation.

Question: Now that God's Spirit has come, are we left deficient in anything?

For Group Discussion:
Look in Romans 5:1–11 (see Day 6) at the things the Holy Spirit brings to us from the cross of Christ, that constitute 'God's love . . . poured into our hearts':

- *while we were still weak, Christ died for the ungodly,*

- *while we were yet sinners, Christ died for us,*

- *while enemies, we were reconciled to God by the death of His Son,*

- *we are now justified by his blood,*

- *we shall be saved by him from the wrath of God,*

- *we shall be saved by his life,*

- *we rejoice in God.*

What more could the Spirit bring to us of love than all of that?
Note in Acts 2:37–47 the things that followed from what the Spirit brought:

- *people were cut to the heart, in a way that demanded that something be done,*

- *they repented,*

- *they were baptised into Jesus Christ,*

- *they received the gift of the Holy Spirit themselves,*

- *they received a promise that was to their children and to others far off,*

- *they were called in to God,*

- *they were saved from their crooked generation,*

- *they were devoted to the apostles' teaching,*

- *they were devoted to fellowship with one another,*

- *they were devoted to the breaking of bread together,*

- *they were devoted to the prayers,*

- *the fear of God came upon them,*

- *many wonders and signs were done,*

- *the believers were together,*

- *they had all things in common,*

- *possessions and goods were sold and distribution was made to the needy,*

- *they attended the temple together,*

- *they shared meals in their homes,*

- *their hearts were glad and generous,*

- *they praised God,*

- *they had favour with all the people,*

- *the Lord added to their number day by day those who were being saved.*

Take any of these things and try to see how they would have flowed from those elements looked at above in Romans 5:1–11.

What differences would it make if these things were operative in our church, or in our community? How could this come to be?

Prayer: *Isaiah 12:2–6.*

Week 24

REPENTANCE AND THE FORGIVENESS
OF SINS

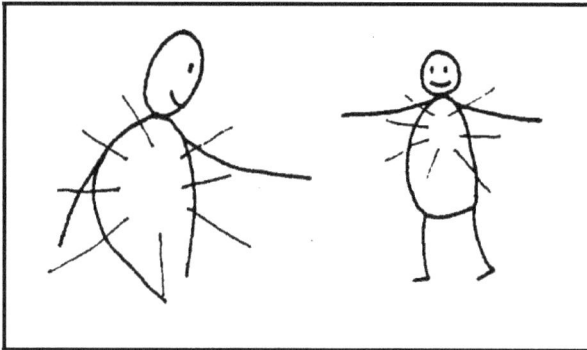

Day 1: Ezekiel 36:22–32

Repentance and the forgiveness of sins go together, and both are a gift from God (see Acts 5:31). Repentance is literally a 'change of mind' or change of attitude, a change of heart. As here in verse 26: 'a new heart I will give you, and a new spirit I will put within you'. This is a forgiven heart—one that is clean from all uncleannesses of sin and idolatry (vv. 25, 29a). It is a warm, palpable, living, human heart, flowing with the good issues of life (v. 26; see Proverbs 4:23; John 7:38), not a cold, hard, dead heart of stone. It is a heart 'after God's own heart' (1 Samuel 13:14). It comes by God's gift of His Holy Spirit (v. 27), bringing to bear in us all the work and life of Christ. It issues in glad and loving obedience to God (v. 27).

We become warmly and intimately related with God (v. 28; see also Jeremiah 31:31–34—the new covenant).

Repentance and forgiveness come as a result of God's kind and gracious blessing (vv. 24, 29–30). Only when we know the greatness of the forgiveness that is there can we truly face the extent of our own evil (vv. 31–32; compare Luke 5:1–11).

Question: Have I accepted the gift of a new, clean, living heart? Have I exercised the gift of repentance?

Day 2: Mark 1:1–15

Jesus' message, as John's before him (see Matthew 3:1–2), was not, 'Repent, because you are all terrible sinners'. It was, 'The *kingdom of God* is at hand; repent, and believe in the gospel' (v. 15). The kingdom of God is a wonderful thing (see, for example, Micah 4:1–4; Isaiah 25:1–12). Who would not want to repent and come right in on it? This is what Jesus is holding out to us. Once again, it is the blessings of God that bring us to true repentance towards Him.

Question: Has the focus of my 'repentance' been more on my sins, or on the goodness and glory of God?

Day 3: Acts 3:1–26

After the Spirit has come, Peter says to the people of Israel, 'Repent, therefore, and turn again, that your sins may be wiped out, so that times of refreshing may come from the presence of the Lord' (v. 19). God has raised Jesus from the dead 'to bless you in turning every one of you from your wickedness' (v. 26). It is a most attractive and heartfelt appeal. Later Peter tells the council the same thing: 'God exalted him [Jesus] at his right hand . . . to *give* repentance to Israel and forgiveness of sins' (Acts 5:31). In Acts 11:18 it is acknowledged that the same gift is given to all the nations. In Acts 17:30 repentance is *commanded* to all people. What more incentive do we need?

To think about: Have I seen repentance as something (like a penance) I must put myself through, or as a joyful gift from God?

Day 4: Psalm 51:1–19

David was 'a man after God's own heart' (1 Samuel 13:14)—he had a heart for God. This psalm is the classic expression of his repentance—clean and strong. There are no excuses, nor any attempt to try and make up for what he has done wrong. His focus is wholly on God. It is *God* who must deal with his sin, wash him, cleanse him, purge him, fill him, restore him and do him good. This prayer is made in confidence that God can do what David could never do for himself. Indeed, that God delights to do this. Without a prayer like this, we are still stuck with our sin, in our pathetic self-serving attempts to put ourselves right. See also Psalm 32:1–11.

To pray about: 'Restore to me the joy of your salvation, and uphold me with a willing spirit' (v. 12).

Day 5: John 13:1–11

Jesus here is washing his disciples' feet, but it also has a deeper meaning (see vv. 3, 7). It relates to the great cleansing that comes to us by his mighty action on the cross and in the resurrection, mediated to us by his word (see Matthew 26:28; John 15:3). It is false pride that stops Peter, and us, from wanting to receive that lovely ministration.

Question: Have I received the total forgiveness of sins?

Day 6: Matthew 18:21–35

The test and true living out of our forgiveness is our forgiving of others. We only do not forgive when we do not know how much we have been forgiven. The reason why the wicked servant was so intent on collecting his debts was that he had no conception of how much he had been forgiven. Each talent amounted to fifteen years' wages of a labourer. This servant owed ten thousand talents—the equivalent to 150,000 years of hard labour. And he still thought that he could work to pay it off! The king had borne all of that, at his own great cost. Yet the servant still would not relent on the equivalent of a mere 100 days' work from a fellow servant. Clearly he had no idea of what had really happened, and his own forgiveness was inoperative. Jesus told us we would not be forgiven if we did not forgive. If we do not forgive, we are then like a full rainwater tank with its tap turned off: it can receive nothing until it turns on and gives out.

To think about: 'Be kind to one another, tenderhearted, forgiving one another, *as God in Christ forgave you*' (Ephesians 4:32).

For Group Discussion:
Read Luke 5:1–11. Imagine yourselves in the position of Simon Peter. What had he been doing before Jesus spoke to him? How would he have felt when Jesus told him to go out fishing again? What would have been going through his mind as he hauled in the catch? What was it that brought about Peter's exclamation in verse 8? Why is there astonishment and fear? Why did Simon respond so readily to the statement that he would now be a catcher of people? What does this teach us about repentance and the forgiveness of sins (see Days 1 and 2)?

What difference does it make to know repentance as a gift from God rather than something we have to do for ourselves (see Day 3)?

Imagine yourselves again in the position of Simon Peter, this time in John 13:5–9 (see Day 5). What is it that makes us say, 'You will never wash my feet'? What makes us change our mind? What do cleansing from sin and belonging to Jesus have to do with each other?

'We only do not forgive when we do not know how much we have been forgiven' (Day 6). Pray for any in the group who may still find it difficult to know forgiveness for themselves and for others.

Prayer: *Psalm 51.*

Week 25

FAITH AND BELONGING TO GOD

Day 1: 1 John 4:13–21

Faith, or believing in God, is a gift from God (see Philippians 1:29: 'it has been *granted* to you that for the sake of Christ you . . . *believe* in him'), a work of the Holy Spirit. By faith is effected our union with God—'by this we know that we abide in him and he in us' (v. 13). It is focussed on Jesus as the Son of God (v. 15). 'We know and believe the love God has for us' as Father (v. 16). It is not enough simply to believe that God exists, though that is part of it (see Hebrews 11:6). Even those directly opposed to God can acknowledge that (see James 2:19). It is an active, relational *trusting* of God in all things, a faith that knows the forgiveness of sins and the love of God (vv. 17–19), and issues in practical love for one another (vv. 20–21; see James 2:14–26; Galatians 5:6—'faith working through love').

Question: Do I know by faith that 'we abide in God, and he in us'?

Day 2: Genesis 15:1–6

Faith is knowing, trusting and loving God in all that He is doing throughout history, centred in the cross and resurrection of His Son. Here Abraham was given a glimpse of part of God's great plan to bring blessing to the nations of the world, and of his own part in it, and he willingly aligned himself with all that God was doing. This was Abraham's faith.

Because what God was doing would culminate (whether Abraham knew it or not) in the giving of His Son on the cross to take away the sin of the world (including Abraham's), then the effect of Abraham's believing was for him to participate in the righteousness or justification from God won for us there. 'He believed the LORD; and he reckoned it to him as righteousness' (v. 6). This did not come by virtue of Abraham's act of faith, but by virtue of the acts of the One in whom he put his faith—the propitiating God (see Romans 4:1–25; Luke 18:9–14).

To think about: What am I looking to in order to make myself right or justify myself in life? Is it my own actions and achievements, or is it the works of God who 'justifies the ungodly' (Romans 4:5)? Is my faith in myself, or is it firmly in the God who made atonement for us all in the blood of His own Son?

Day 3: Habakkuk 2:1–4

The prophet Habakkuk lived in a time (about 600 BC) when evil appeared to triumph and all was destruction and violence. He sought the Lord about this, and was given a classic designation of faith that was later taken up in the New Testament (see Romans 1:17; Galatians 3:11; Hebrews 10:38–39). Faith, the only true way to live, is being upright and straightforward with God as He really is.

Isaiah was given similar indications in similarly disruptive times: 'In returning and rest you shall be saved; in quietness and trust shall be your strength' (Isaiah 30:15). We constantly reject that, to speed off on our own way, and need to be reminded, 'The one who believes will not be in haste [*or* panic]' (Isaiah 28:16).

To think about: 'We have a strong city; he sets up salvation as walls and bulwarks. Open the gates, that the righteous nation which keeps faith may enter in. You keep in perfect peace the one whose mind is stayed on you, because he trusts in you. Trust in the LORD for ever, for the LORD GOD is an everlasting rock' (Isaiah 26:1–4).

Day 4: Romans 3:20–28

In contrast to the condemnation that the law of God brings on all of us who have not kept it, the gift of faith in God brings us justification and righteousness before God on account of what God has done in Christ. To be justified is to be freed from guilt, free to love and obey God. Paul says, 'I am not ashamed of the gospel: it is the power of God for salvation to every one who has faith'. 'In it', he says, 'the righteousness of God is revealed through faith for faith' (Romans 1:16–17). Only those who have faith will see this salvation, and they will see that it comes to those who have faith, a faith that increases from strength to strength.

To pray about: 'That I may gain Christ and be found in him, not having a righteousness of my own, based on law, but that which is through faith in Christ, the righteousness from God that depends on faith' (Philippians 3:8–9).

Day 5: Hebrews 10:32 – 11:3

Faith has to do with endurance (v. 36)—knowing that God is constant to the end, and staying with Him no matter what; knowing that in Him we have 'a better possession and an abiding one' (v. 34). The things of God that we believe in and hope for will not always appear to be so. 'We walk by faith, not by sight' (2 Corinthians 5:7). But such is the confidence in God that we have been given, that we have in our faith 'the *assurance* of things hoped for, the *conviction* of things not seen' (11:1).

To think about: Is there any other way we can truly live, apart from faith in God?

Day 6: Hebrews 11:4–16

Here is set before us the goal of all our faith: the heavenly city prepared by God, our true homeland where we already belong as we head towards it, our solid and lasting inheritance, promised to us by God. This is what has propelled the people of faith throughout the ages, through times of not knowing and not reaching, through opposition and death. But once we know God, where else can we be?

To think about: Are we counting on God's faithfulness to us in all His promises?

For Group Discussion:

*What is the difference between believing **that** something is so and believing **in** a person? What difference does it make to us to experience faith as a relationship rather than simply as an intellectual assent (see Day 1)?*

Faith is personal. It is also huge. Think of Abraham looking at the stars, and being shown the whole plan and purpose of God, and being asked to assent to his appointed part in it (Genesis 15:1–6, Day 2). Some of us may have experienced God's faithfulness in the relatively small matters of our lives. Let members of the group relate these experiences, and then try to see how these fit into God's larger plan and purpose.

The battle of faith is constantly between accepting and trusting in God's own righteous actions towards us, and our insistence on trying to get things right for ourselves. Let members of the group share instances of this battle in their own lives (see Days 3 and 4).

'You have need of endurance, so that you may do the will of God and receive what is promised' (Hebrews 10:36). Often our 'faith' has its cut-out points. What are some of the things that may cause people to 'lose' their faith?

How much is this connected with the extent to which we are maintaining our own agenda, or are participating in God's agenda, with God's ultimate goal in view (see Days 5 and 6)?

Prayer*: Psalm 18:1–19.*

Week 26

THE FRUIT OF THE SPIRIT

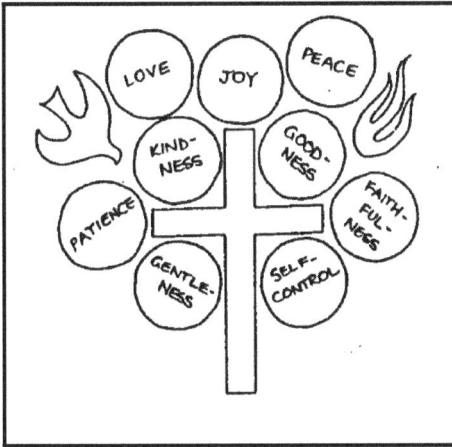

Day 1: John 3:1–21

Never despise the notion of being 'born again'. Jesus said we cannot even see, let alone enter, God's kingdom without the new birth (vv. 3, 5). This comes through believing in Jesus as the one sent from God to be lifted up on the cross as the pure embodiment of our sin and evil, for our healing, to save us from eternal death (vv. 13–17; compare Numbers 21:4–9; John 1:12–13). The new birth is literally 'from above'—it is an action of God by the Spirit, who brings the cleansing of forgiveness (v. 5) and relates us to God as His children. It is a transformation. Formerly we were depending upon ourselves and our own (God-given) flesh as the basis of our operations, over against God. Now we are brought to a new and continuing dependence upon God's Spirit in all things (vv. 6–8). It is a discovery that all our true good works are those wrought in us by God through the Spirit (v. 21).

Question: Have I been born again from above by the Spirit of God?

Day 2: Galatians 3:1–14

If the new birth comes from God, then the new life that follows it, with all that it entails, must no less also come from God. We cannot begin with the Spirit and not continue in the Spirit. To return to our own flesh as the base of our operations, apart from or over against God—to attempt to 'go it alone' or 'do it ourselves'—is a denial of all that God has done for us in Christ, and a return to the way of condemnation. So, having begun by believing, we have no other way to continue but by faith—that is, faith in God and His action for us and in us by Christ through the Spirit.

To think about: Why would we ever want to do it any other way?

Day 3: Galatians 5:16–26

'The desires of the flesh' here does not mean that all fleshly desires are wrong, and that we have to escape them by becoming 'spiritual' in some airy-fairy sense. Not at all. Our flesh and its inbuilt desires are part of the wonderful gift to us from God, designed to be lived in dependence upon God and in union with Him. It is when we cease to regard it as a gift, and begin to use it as the base of our own operations, apart from and over against our Father, that our flesh becomes a perverse and hostile entity, which has no part in the kingdom or rule of God. 'If one turns away his ear from hearing the law [of God], even his prayer is an abomination' (Proverbs 28:9). It is from this monstrosity that 'the works of the flesh' emerge, as listed in verses 19–21. Far more to be desired are the strong and gentle 'fruit of the Spirit' (vv. 22–24), wrought by God in those who know that as sinners they have been crucified, judged, condemned, put to death and raised to new life in Christ. These good things—springing from the law of God written on our hearts by the Holy Spirit (see Jeremiah 31:33; Ezekiel 36:27)—are truly the fruit in us of Christ's cross.

To think about: 'If we live [have been brought to life] by the Spirit, let us also walk [continue to live day by day] by the Spirit' (v. 25).

Day 4: Ephesians 2:1–10

'And we humbly beseech you, heavenly Father, so to assist us with your grace, that we may continue in that holy fellowship, and do all such good works as you have prepared for us to walk in' (*A Prayer Book for Australia*, p. 115). The connections between that prayer and this passage are obvious. Isn't it good that even our good works are ready, waiting for us, prepared for us by God! That takes a lot of the pressure off us—we are simply to walk in God's ways by glad and loving faith, day by day.

To think about: Is there really any other way to go? 'For the ways of the LORD are right, and the upright walk *in them*, but transgressors stumble *in them*' (Hosea 14:9). It is not as if there are two ways. There is only the one way of the Lord, which is right, and we either walk in it freely and gladly, or we make heavy weather of it.

Day 5: Colossians 2:16 – 3:4

Even after we have been born anew, it seems the flesh still tries to remain very active in its own 'right', trying to convince us that we can do it by our own might. This takes many shapes and forms, from superstitious practices through to legalistic rituals or habitual patterns of behaviour. These sometimes look very pious or 'holy', but are nothing more than the self-centred flesh indulging itself in unchecked self-aggrandisement. The counter to that is always only: 'I have been crucified with Christ. My life now belongs to God in Him. He is my best and only hope.'

To think about: 'You have died, and your life is hidden with Christ in God'.

Day 6: Colossians 3:5–17

All our actions now are to come from the new nature that we have put on in Christ to take after our Father. Why are we not to lie? Not primarily because 'lying is bad', but because it no longer fits with who we are now in him who is the Truth (see v. 9). Christ is now the determinant of all our actions. Governed by the peace (forgiveness) of Christ, which comes to us by the rich indwelling of Christ's gospel word, we are to 'do everything in the name of the Lord Jesus, giving thanks to God the Father through him'.

To think about: What are the implications of the fruit of the Spirit (love, joy, peace, patience, kindness, goodness, faithfulness, gentleness, self-control) for our relationships now with others?

For Group Discussion:

The thrust of this week's readings is this: We are created as human beings to live only ever by the Spirit, always in dependence upon God. This is how we live up to our true stature as human beings in the image of God. We have taken our wonderful God-given flesh, and foolishly and deliberately set it up as the base of our operations over against God—a doomed and unworkable strategy that gives rise to all kinds of hell-bent works of evil. This is called living 'according to the flesh'. God in His faithful holy love has given His Son to the hell of the cross, to free us from these evil works and their necessary condemnation, and to take us on into living with Him in the Spirit by faith. This is called being 'born again' from above. Even so, having begun now in the Spirit, we can still try to go on in the flesh. Against this the Spirit constantly opposes the word of the cross, the message of our liberation, to keep us in the ways of God's holy law, which is the fruit of the Spirit's work in us, in that strong and loving dependence on God that is the gift of faith.

It is important that we help each other understand this, as we so easily misconstrue or distort it. For instance, we can think of the new birth as somehow bringing us into a 'spiritual' realm, detached from the 'earthly'. This is an evasion of the very earthy issues that true holiness brings us into. Or we can say we are now freed from any requirements of the law of God, to live how we please. This evades the responsibility we have for what we are and do—it still does not understand the true nature of the law as the way of God's own being and action, in which we are to participate fully.

Let members of the group each take one of the elements enumerated as 'the fruit of the Spirit' in Galatians 5:22–23, and say how this has been an issue for them in their lives.

Prayer: *Psalm 119:145–152.*

Week 27

THE GIFTS OF THE SPIRIT

Day 1: 2 Corinthians 10:3–6

In this present age, in which Jesus our Lord is putting down under his feet everything that opposes God's kingdom (see 1 Corinthians 15:20–28, Week 18, Day 1; also Ephesians 1:19–23), there is a fierce battle raging. Who of us is equal to these things, or can see our way clearly to what is really happening? How are we to play our part in this great spiritual warfare? Only by the Spirit of God, and the *necessary* gifts that he brings, can we have 'divine power to destroy strongholds' of evil powers and stubborn human pride.

Question: Am I relying on my own resources to set things right and bring people to Christ, or am I depending always only upon the Spirit of God?

Day 2: 1 Corinthians 12:1–6

We cannot even say from the heart, 'Jesus is Lord!' except by revelation and inspiration of the Holy Spirit. There are other spiritual forces abroad—not least our own stubborn flesh—which may lead us to the opposite conclusion; that is, 'Jesus be cursed!' In our weakness and gullibility we need to know that:

> God our Father is working full bore,
> Jesus is serving us—like we've never been served before!
> Holy Spirit has gifts to outpour,
> And no one can say, 'Jesus is Lord',
> Except by the Holy Spirit!
> (Martin Bleby, *New Creation Hymn Book,* no. 285.)

Question: Do I see God as alive and active here now, or do I think it is all really up to me?

Day 3: 1 Corinthians 12:7–11, 27–30

God is the generous Giver. This list of gifts is by no means all-inclusive (see also Romans 12:6–8; Ephesians 4:7–16; James 3:17; 1 Peter 4:7–11). They are designated in various ways: 'spiritual gifts' (1 Corinthians 12:1, literally 'spirituals'—things or persons inspired by the Spirit); 'gifts' (v. 4, Greek: *charismata*, from which we get 'charismatic renewal'); 'service' (v. 5); 'working' (v. 6); 'manifestation of the Spirit' (v. 7, demonstrations of the Spirit's presence and power). All these names indicate that they have their origin in God. Not all members of the church exercise every gift (vv. 28–30). But gifts of some kind are given to each member. They are not optional extras.

The gifts of the Spirit are not natural endowments, though they are often extensions of that. They are supernatural endowments from God to enable us to know and say and do things we otherwise would not be capable of, for the service of one another in the great cause of God's kingdom. Most of these we see operating in the life and ministry of Jesus (see Week 21, e.g. John 4:16–19: utterance of knowledge; Acts 20:35: utterance of wisdom; Mark 5:35–39: faith; John 14:24: constant prophecy, that is, speaking of words from God; plus numerous healings and miracles. Often we are exercising these gifts without even being conscious of it: for example, discernment of spirits (see 1 John 2:18–27), when we 'sense' something that is good, or something that is not quite right. They are generally given on occasions when they are needed rather than as permanent endowments, and they are never given for self-aggrandisement, but rather for service of others, to build one another up in the cause of the rule of God.

To think about: What gifts of the Spirit have been operating in my life and ministry?

Day 4: 1 Corinthians 14:1–25

This chapter tells us everything we need to know about the controversial 'gift of tongues', and emphasises the primary importance of prophecy (speaking the word of the Lord). A heart that is filled with the Holy Spirit will want to speak out the wonderful works of God (Acts 2:4–11). Sometimes this will come out in sounds or a 'language' unknown to the speaker—whether an earthly or a heavenly language (see

1 Corinthians 13:1)—but always under the control of the speaker (see 1 Corinthians 14:32; Romans 8:16; this is what distinguishes it from other forms of 'possession' as in 1 Corinthians 12:2–3). Here the rational mind is bypassed (vv. 14–15) as expression is given to the deeper things of the spirit—not always a bad thing. But it is a personal gift for use in private prayer with God (vv. 2, 4). When used publicly, it must always be accompanied by the gift of interpretation, so that others may be edified (vv. 5, 6–19, 27–28). But 'tongues' can also be a sign of judgment, concealing God's word from those who will not believe (vv. 21–22, quoting from Isaiah 28:11–12).

Prophecy, here advocated by Paul as the 'higher' or preferred gift (while not opposed to tongues, see vv. 5, 18, 39), is the speaking to others of intelligible words from God, for their 'upbuilding and encouragement and consolation' (v. 3), in a way that brings benefit and instruction to others (vv. 6, 19). It can also have the function of convicting unbelievers to bring them face to face with the living God (vv. 24–25).

To think about: Truly the church is not left lacking in anything that is needful, by the One who fills all in all (Ephesians 1:19–23)!

Day 5: 1 Corinthians 14:26–33

If all these gifts are available and necessary, then we should exercise them when we come together as a church. Our 'liturgies' need to provide opportunities for the sharing of these dynamic gifts, under right authority and in good order (see v. 40).

To think about: How does Paul's description of worship here differ from our regular church services? How can we encourage the sharing of spiritual gifts?

Day 6: 1 Corinthians 12:31 – 13:13

This classic passage on love is really, as we can see now from its context, an instruction on how the spiritual gifts are to be exercised. Gifts of the Spirit are all part of the action of *God's love* that is poured into our hearts by the Holy Spirit in the revelation of Christ crucified and risen (see Romans 5:1–11), and so need to be used accordingly. God still gives His gifts even when we use them sinfully (see Matthew 5:45; Romans 11:29)—the coming through of gifts is no necessary indication of virtue or piety! But when they are used in a wrong way, those who use them amount to nothing, and their ministry is ineffectual and worthless (vv. 1–3). Verses 4–7 describe the love of God as set forth in Christ, which is the source and goal of all the gifts of God. The gifts of the Spirit are to be used in this age to build one another up and serve the rule of Christ. For the day is coming when we shall be face to face with the Father, knowing all His love—and then the gifts we have known and used here will be needed no more (vv. 8–13)!

Question: Am I earnestly desiring the higher gifts, and walking in the more excellent way of love?

For Group Discussion:
Here are lists of the various gifts from the passages referred to on Day 3:

<u>1 Corinthians 12</u>
utterance of wisdom
utterance of knowledge
faith
gifts of healing
working of miracles
prophecy
discernment of spirits
tongues
interpretation of tongues
apostles
prophets
teachers
helpers
administrators

<u>James 3</u>
wisdom from above

<u>Romans 12</u>
prophecy
service
teaching
exhortation
contributing
leading
acts of compassion

<u>Ephesians 4</u>
apostles
prophets
evangelists
pastors and teachers

<u>1 Peter 4</u>
speaking the word of God
serving in God's strength

Let members of the group each choose one or two of these gifts from God, and say how they have seen them operating in their own lives or in the lives of others.

What difference would it make for these gifts to be operating in our churches and communities as a matter of course? How can we encourage their use?

How can we guard against using the gifts without love?

Prayer: *Ephesians 3:14–21.*

THE CHURCH AND THE
KINGDOM OF GOD

Weeks 28–36

Week 28

THE PLANNED FAMILY

Day 1: Ephesians 3:14–21

God is *Father* (Greek: *pater*). It is the nature of the Father to have a *family* (Greek: *patria*) of many children. The reason God created us, and everything that is, was so He could have a wonderful family and a home for the family to live in, and so set forth the glories of His true nature as Father. So it is from the Father that all families and family relationships are derived and patterned.

It is not the family that makes the Father, but the Father who makes the family. How could God be Father before He had any children? God has always been Father—of the Son. He is 'the God and Father of our Lord Jesus Christ' (Ephesians 1:3). So the forming of the family of God will only ever be through the one and only Son. It will be by us coming into the Son himself and so into that wonderful relationship that he has with the Father. This is what will unite 'every family in heaven and on earth' into the one family of God (see Ephesians 1:10). Hence Paul prays that all the riches of Christ in his love-relationship with the Father may be engendered in us.

Question: How large a view do I have of 'family'? Where does my little family stand in relation to the Father of all, and the family of God (see Mark 3:31–35; 10:29–30; Matthew 10:21, 34–39)?

Day 2: Ephesians 1:3–10

Here we see the plan of God—how the Father has planned His family from 'before the foundation of the world'. As we would expect, the children are to be 'like father, like son'; that is, 'holy and blameless'. How can this be for us who are sinners? Does this for ever count us out as part of God's family? Paul goes on to say how this can be. We are destined to be 'sons' (inclusive) *through Jesus Christ*; that is, through *the* Son. This will be by the *grace* God has bestowed on us in him: redemption through the cross, forgiveness, union with Christ.

Question: Am I content to be just the muddle-headed sinner that I am in my own little setting, or has my heart been gripped by this high and noble calling?

Day 3: Revelation 7:1–17

Here are two pictures of the one thing—the whole family of God at the end-time. The first picture (vv. 1–8) is in terms of the great nation of Israel. It was through the choice and appointment of Israel that God, through covenant, began to form His worldwide family. But in the New Testament the whole people of God is seen as the new 'Israel of God' (Galatians 6:15–16), and this is what is referred to here. The designation of the tribes and the one hundred and forty-four thousand (not necessarily to be taken literally) signify a very large and complete number of people who belong to God, who are 'sealed' or marked with the name of the Father and the Son (see Revelation 14:1).

The second picture (vv. 9–17) shows us the same reality from another perspective, and tells us some more about it. They are indeed without number, from every ethnic grouping in the world. How can they come to be there? Only by the cleansing from sin and the powerful purity of action that has come through the shedding of Christ's blood on the cross (v. 14; see also Revelation 19:8). This is why they cry out in praise of God's mighty act of salvation, according to His glorious plan (vv. 10–12). What a magnificent Fatherly goodness is manifested in all who are there (vv. 15–17)!

To think about: An article of clothing marked with my name belongs to me. Have I been marked with the name of the Father and the Son? Have I and my deeds been washed in the blood of the Lamb? What then is my destiny?

Day 4: Hebrews 2:10–18

Who is 'he for whom all things exist'? The Father. What is He doing? 'Bringing many sons [inclusive] to glory'. How does He do this? Through one called 'the pioneer of their salvation'—the one who makes and leads the way—who is made perfect (brought to fullness or completeness) through suffering. He originates from the Father as the eternal Son (as we have originated from the Father as the created sons, inclusive). He is our brother who has entered into our flesh and our human condition. In his own flesh he has brought our guilt to judgment and destroyed the power the devil has over us by fear of death and judgment (see Hebrews 9:27). He is the one who can truly say, 'Here am I, and the children God has given me' (v. 13).

To think about: Isaiah 53:10–11 says: 'When he makes himself an offering for sin, *he shall see his offspring,* he shall prolong his days: the will of the LORD shall prosper in his hand; he shall see the fruit of the travail of his soul and be satisfied'. The family of God is forged through Christ's cross. Was not this 'the joy that was set before him', for which he 'endured the cross, despising the shame' (Hebrews 12:2)?

Day 5: Isaiah 43:1–7

This sets out the sureness of God's purpose regarding His sons and daughters. They are formed and summoned by the action of God—by His redemption and calling—and so nothing will stand in the way of their coming together as God's family, and nothing will be too much trouble to bring all this to pass. Why? 'Because you are precious in my eyes, and honoured, and *I love you.*' Amazing grace! This is 'the people whom I formed for myself that they might declare my praise' (v. 21).

To think about: Do I believe verse 2? What experience have I had of that already? Am I a part of the covenant family? What confidence does that give me to cease timidity and exercise the 'spirit of power and love and self-control' (2 Timothy 1:7)?

Day 6: Romans 8:18–25

Everything hangs on the coming of the family of God. The vast creation, intended to be our glorious home, was 'subjected to futility' by God as a result of human sin (see Genesis 3:17–19). Its destiny is intimately tied up in ours. Now it awaits 'the revealing of the sons of God' for it to be able to be released from bondage and participate in 'the glorious liberty of the children of God'. The family of God will come into its own at the glorious resurrection of the dead (v. 23).

Question: Have I attempted to accommodate myself to things as they are now, 'subjected to futility', or am I living in hope of 'the redemption of our bodies'?

For Group Discussion:
'It is from the Father that all families and family relationships are derived and patterned' (Day 1). We have also seen that relationships now participate in the frustration and futility

that has come on account of human sin and evil. Let members of the group share some experiences of family living, both positive and negative. What would it mean for these relationships to be set free into 'the glorious liberty of the children of God' (Romans 8:21, Day 6), and for us to be united with all things in Christ (see Ephesians 1:10, Days 1 and 2)?

What sort of things do we do in families to secure ourselves against other people and the outside world? What is the vision of God's family in Revelation 7 (Day 3)? How do we move from one to the other?

How can we encourage one another in the truth of God's words to His people in Isaiah 43:4: 'you are precious in my eyes, and honoured, and I love you'?

Prayer: *Revelation 4:8b, 11; 5:9–10, 12, 13b.*

Week 29

CALLED TO GOD—SENT TO SERVE

Day 1: Genesis 12:1–3

God's great plan of salvation, to bring a people to Himself, began with Abraham and Sarah. From the beginning the principles of His operation amongst us were made clear—the twofold reason for our existence as the people of God:

- 'I will *bless* you . . .' (v. 2). First of all God wanted a special people who would know Him and enjoy His blessings. But this was not just for our own sake, but for the sake of others also whom God calls to Himself;

- '. . . so that you will *be a blessing* . . . and in you all the families of the earth shall be blessed' (vv. 2–3).

Abraham's calling and blessing was not just for himself alone, nor just for the nation of Israel that would come from him, but for all the nations of the world.

Question: How much do we see ourselves to exist as a church only for our own comfort and reassurance as members? To what extent do we see ourselves as being here for the sake of those still outside? Do we see ourselves as those through whom the blessings of God are to come to all the nations?

Day 2: Romans 9:1–26

Some are troubled that the selection and choosing of some by God in the process of salvation appears to exclude others—as if they have some 'right' which is being denied. The fact is that all the nations, including Abraham's family, had *already excluded themselves* from God's blessings by their rejection of God, their sin and their idolatry (see Genesis chs 3 – 11; Ephesians 2:11–12). The call of Abraham and the people of God through the ages simply serves to emphasise this fact. That is what makes the nations so angry about it (see e.g. Psalm 2). Any 'inclusion' of anyone by God is an amazing act of undeserved grace. That the blessings are so full and so free highlights the great love and wonder of this glorious grace.

Here Paul enumerates the rich blessings given to Israel (vv. 4–5), and expresses his deep anguish at his fellow-Jews' non-appreciation of these blessings in his own day (vv. 1–3), as evidenced by their widespread rejection of Jesus as Messiah and Son of God. But he points out the personal *selectivity* of God's mode of operation down through the history of Israel, according to His compassion and mercy (vv. 6–16). This also involves the hardening of hearts that insist on remaining obdurate towards Him (God will never harden a heart that is soft towards Him), for the purpose of making His glory and love for His people more widely known, according to His sovereign purpose (vv. 17–18).

In our perverse self-righteous way we still ask, 'Why does He still find fault?' God finds no fault that is not already there. It is in the face of all the faults of the whole human race that His grace makes inexorable headway to bring many to glory—not just from Israel but from all the nations (vv. 19–24). It was ever His intention to make a people out of those who would have nothing to do with Him, and a family out of those who had rejected His Fatherhood (vv. 20–26; see also Luke 15:11–32).

To think about: Do I somehow think that God 'owes me a living'? Or am I glad to be a lump of clay moulded by the Potter (vv. 20–24)?

Day 3: Isaiah 49:1–7

This is one of many passages in the Old and New Testaments which insist that the destiny of the people of God is intimately tied up with the purposes of God for all the nations. It is made clear time and again that God's concern, focussed on Israel and the church, was never for Israel and the church alone, but for the ends of the earth (vv. 6–7). Time and again Israel declined from this great calling (see e.g. the Book of Jonah), and in its own life refused to walk in God's way. This prophecy speaks of a servant of God, 'one deeply despised, abhorred by the nations' (v. 7), who comes from Israel to bring Israel back to God, and so goes on to fulfil Israel's destiny as 'a light to the nations' (vv. 5–6).

Jesus was recognised as this one at the time of his birth (see Luke 2:22–35).

Question: Do I know myself to be a part of this servant of God: called by God from the womb (v. 1), dependent for all things on him (v. 4), prepared as a weapon of God to take His word of love and blessing to the nations (vv. 2–3, 5–7)?

Day 4: Mark 3:13–19

In his appointment of twelve apostles (corresponding to the twelve tribes of Israel, see Luke 22:28–30), Jesus is reconstituting a new Israel for the next stage of God's plan— the going out of the word of the gospel to all the nations. Note that the same foundation principles are evident as at the call of Abraham (v. 14, see Day 1):

- 'to be *with* him'; that is, to know him and to enjoy the blessings of his presence, his love, his teaching, and his healing power,

- 'to be *sent out* to preach and have authority to cast out demons'. In other words, to bring the blessings of God into the lives of other people. This is why they were called 'apostles', which means, 'those who are sent out'.

To think about: We say in the Nicene Creed, 'We believe in one holy catholic and apostolic church'. 'Catholic' ('according to the whole') means here the whole truth of the whole people of God for the whole world, and 'apostolic' means not only that we uphold the apostles' teaching, but also that we go with it into the whole world as part of the 'sending out' that began with them. Am I a living part of the one, holy, catholic and apostolic church?

Day 5: Romans 11:7–24

Some are still troubled by the notion of God's 'hardening' action. However, this remains a fact of life, as Paul the apostle knew only too well. Here he shows how the hardening serves to further the purposes of God's kingdom for all the nations, and works to fulfil God's promises even to those who have been hardened for a time—in spite of themselves! The rejection of Paul by fellow Jews in the synagogues (see e.g. Acts 13:38–52) drove him to share the gospel with the Gentile nations. This was in fulfilment of his original call from Christ (Acts 26:16–18). When the Jews see the Gentiles taking up the rich blessings of their inheritance that they have rejected, will this not move them to desire these more earnestly (v. 11)? Meanwhile promises made to Israel still stand (see 11:29), and when they reach their fulfilment, as they surely will, together with the Gentiles who have been brought in through Israel's stubbornness, what unimaginable riches will be there (vv. 12–16)! God's dealings in this way with His people Israel should serve to make us Gentiles stand in awe, never to presume upon the great mercy that has come to us, and never to despise any who at this time may be stumbling in hardness or unbelief (vv. 17–24).

Question: To what extent do we trust in ourselves that we are righteous and despise others (see Luke 18:9–14)? What is the antidote to that? What is the truth of God's mercy to me (see 11:32)?

Day 6: Romans 11:25–36

Why have we ever thought that we might be able to do a better job of running the world than God has? When could we ever match the grandeur, the sovereignty, the severity and the kindness of His great and glorious mercy and grace in the face of obdurate human hatred and sin? And to think and know that *we* are now in that awesome mercy!

Pray: Romans 11:33–36.

For Group Discussion:
Have someone in the group read again slowly, with pauses, Isaiah 49:1–7 (see Day 3), and let members of the group each hear these words as their own personal calling in Christ. After a time of quiet meditation, let members of the group say what came through to them, and what difference that could now make in their lives.

Do the same with Mark 3:13–19. Imagine yourselves to be among those called to Jesus, to be with him (the privilege and thrill of that!), and to be sent out (the excitement and dread of that!). Think of particular people or groups that he is sending you to.

Share and pray together for the particular people and groups to whom you are sent.

Prayer: *Psalm 2.*

Week 30

CHRIST AND HIS CHURCH

Day 1: Daniel 7:1–28

In the midst of the terrible rampages of earthly empires as they rise and fall, God as the everlasting 'Ancient of Days' has set His eternal throne. He gives final and enduring authority over 'all peoples, nations, and languages' to '*one like a son of man*'; that is, the true human being (vv. 13–14). 'Son of man' was the title that Jesus consistently applied to himself (see e.g. Matthew 8:20; 12:8; 16:13–16; 20:17–19; 24:29–31; 26:63–64). Dominion is given to him in the midst of great judgment. But he is not alone. Dominion and kingdom is also given at the same time to '*the saints of the Most High*'; that is, all those who belong to the holy God (vv. 18, 27). They are one with the Son of man in his victory and his glory, and he is one with them. 'Here am I, and the children God has given me' (Hebrews 2:13).

Question: Does Jesus ever consider himself apart from the ones he loves and the ones he died to save? Is that how I see him now?

Day 2: John 15:1–8

Jesus is the True Vine. The 'vine' in the Old Testament was a corporate image—it stood for the whole of God's people Israel (see Isaiah 5:1–7; Psalm 80:8–19). Jesus is the True Vine because Israel has been a false and unfruitful vine—unfaithful to God and subjected to God's judgment. 'My Father is the vinedresser'—the one who comes with a sharp knife to bring judgment on the vine (see Isaiah 5:5–6; Psalm 80:12). Note that Jesus is not saying, 'I am the trunk of the vine, and you are joined to me as branches'. No—Jesus is the *whole vine*, and in that vine we are his branches. So when the vinedresser's knife comes, it falls first of all on Jesus himself. Jesus is talking about God's action in him on the cross (see Mark 14:27; Zechariah 13:7), and our place in that. Jesus has been sent from the Father, so to identify himself with us in mighty love that, when the final terrible judgment on our sinfulness is made, *Jesus is there* bearing it in us and for us, and we are there in him (see John 12:31–33; 2 Corinthians 5:14–15). In this fearful action we are to *abide in him* by faith. It is in this crucible of the cross that the church, the true new humanity, is formed. If we abide in him, through faith in the cleansing truth of the cross (v. 3), then the effect of the Father's judgment in our lives will be to prune and cleanse us and make us fruitful (vv. 2b–5). If we do not abide in Christ, in who he is and what he has come to do, then when that knife falls it will cut us off so that we wither and die and are destroyed (for we are as good as dead already). The final bar of judgment is the cross of Christ.

To think about: Do I want to abide in Christ in the action of the cross, or in some other more cosy way? Is there really any other way available to me?

Day 3: Ephesians 2:11–22

At the time of the call of Abraham, all the nations, including Abraham's family, were unclean in God's sight (see Week 29, Day 2). God in love and mercy selected the nation of Israel to know Him, and gave them 'the law of commandments and ordinances' (v. 15). One function of this law was to teach Israel 'to make a distinction between the unclean and the clean'. The effect of this was to separate Israel from the Gentile nations and their uncleanness: 'You shall be holy to me; for I the LORD am holy, and have separated you from the peoples, that you should be mine' (see Leviticus 11:46–47; 20:22–26). Now that a great cleansing has been effected in the cross, not only for Israel but for all the nations, that 'dividing wall of hostility' has been broken down (see Acts 10:9–20, 34–35). Both Israel and the Gentile nations together are now reconciled to God in the peace of that forgiveness and cleansing wrought in Christ's blood, and together are 'members of the household [family] of God', a dwelling place fit for the Lord of hosts (see Psalm 24)! The new humanity, the 'one new man', is minted in the cross.

To think about: Is our 'peace' with one another just a tolerant getting along with each other, or is it something deeper?

Day 4: Acts 26:4–23

This is Paul's account of his own conversion to Christ. He has not been persecuting Jesus himself, who by now has risen and ascended, but those who belong to Jesus. Yet Jesus himself says to Paul in the vision, 'I am Jesus, *whom you are persecuting*' (v. 15). So closely does Jesus identify with himself those for whom he has died. Is this where Paul first encountered the reality of the church as Christ's own body? We are one with the present humanity of the risen and ascended and glorified Jesus.

To think about: 'He has passed beyond our sight, not to abandon us but to be our hope, that where he is we might also be and reign with him in glory' (*An Australian Prayer Book,* pp. 168–9).

Day 5: 1 Corinthians 12:12–27

This passage has to do with mutual relationships and ministries within the one 'body of Christ'. Christ is 'the head of the body, the church' (Colossians 1:18; as he is 'head over all things for the church, which is his body', Ephesians 1:22–23), and Christ is the body as a whole, of which we are parts. Note the special care accorded to the 'weaker', 'less honourable', 'unpresentable' parts, who are indispensable to the whole body. The church is never meant to be a fellowship only of the 'spiritually strong'. The dynamic of mutual dependence and care is essential to the love of Christ.

To think about: Have I ever committed the twin errors of saying either, 'I do not belong to the body', or, 'I have no need of you'?

Day 6: John 10:11–30

Just as Jesus said he was the True Vine, over against false and faithless Israel, so here he is the Good (or authentic) Shepherd, over against the false 'shepherds' (rulers) of Israel (see John 9:34; compare Ezekiel 34). The mark of our true Leader is his willingness to put the good of those he serves before his own selfish interests. In this he mirrors, and is one with, the love of the Father from whom he has come.

To think about: What could be more securing for us than verses 27–29? What have you known of the Good Shepherd's hand in your own life?

For Group Discussion:
Begin with John 10:11–30 (Day 6). Let members of the group speak of ways in which they have known Jesus acting as the Good Shepherd in their lives.

'One has died for all; therefore all have died. And he died for all, so that those who live might live no longer for themselves, but for him who died and was raised for them' (2 Corinthians 5:14–15, see Day 2). Starting from this statement

by Paul on 'the love of Christ', ask: How did Jesus identify himself with us? How have we been identified with him? What are the implications of that for our present relationship with Jesus?

If we have been cleansed as a whole new humanity in the fiery furnace of the cross, what is the 'peace' we now have with each other (see Day 3)? How does this come through in our experience?

In what ways have we said in the church either, 'I do not belong to the body' (perhaps from a sense of inferiority), or, 'I have no need of you' (perhaps from a sense of superiority)? (See 1 Corinthians 12:15–16, 21, Day 5.) What is the antidote to that?

Prayer: *Psalm 24.*

Week 31

LOVING ONE ANOTHER

Day 1: Ephesians 4:1–6

The heart of all love is the 'one God and Father of us all, who is above all and through all and in all'. He is one in love with the 'one Lord' and the 'one Spirit'. Love is the life of the Trinity—not as a mutual, cosy glow, but love-in-action, purposeful and directed, flowing out to all, and bringing in all in love. It follows then for us, that to love is to live consistently in that love-action of the Trinity. Here Paul tells us to do just that—to live in the unity of the Godhead's love-action that is brought to us by the Spirit.

To think about: Love is something that is *given*. It comes from God, not from us. Paul here does not tell us to make or build the unity of the Spirit, but to *maintain* the unity of the Spirit in the bond of peace—as something already there! What is the difference?

Day 2: John 15:9–17

The new commandment, which goes with the new covenant, is the summary and fulfilment of all the commandments under the old covenant (see Romans 13:8–10; James 2:8; Matthew 5:17–20; 22:34–40). It is the commandment, 'Love one another'. The measure of this love is to be the love of our Father Himself, as experienced by the Son. This love has been fully set forth and made freely available in the Son, in the action of the cross (vv. 9, 12–13). Now we are to live fully and freely as friends of Christ by obeying his command to love, so that our joy in the Father's pleasure may be as full as his.

To think about: It has been said that the distinctive thing about Christian love is that it includes love of *enemies* (see Matthew 5:43–48; Luke 6:27–36). Why should that be so? (Compare Romans 5:6–11.)

Day 3: Ephesians 4:22 – 5:2

Love is living towards others in the forgiveness of God. We only know the depths of God's love when we know the depths of God's forgiveness of us. Then we have no grounds for holding back love from any other person. The love that we have been made for, which comes to us from God in whose image we are made, can now flow freely to others (see 4:32; 5:1–2).

The church is that gathering of forgiven sinners who belong by faith to Jesus Christ, as children of the Father, filled with the Spirit, together in love of God and one another.

The new life comes from 'the new nature, created after the likeness of God' (4:24). This, and not some attempt to follow new rules and principles, is the rationale for Christian living and loving. Why are we to speak the truth (4:25)? Not primarily because lying is wrong, but because the truth is that God has made us 'members of one another', and speaking untruth is not consistent with that reality. Note how the thief is not just to stop stealing, but to come into a position where a change has been made from taking to giving (4:28). This is consistent with the nature of God. So also we are not just to refrain from 'evil talk'; we are to give out that which edifies and imparts grace (4:29).

To grieve the 'Holy Spirit of God' does not drive him away from us. It is because *he is still there in us* that he can be grieved by our sin. That is what makes it all the more awful.

To think about: 'Walk in love, as Christ loved us and gave himself up for us, a fragrant offering and sacrifice to God' (5:2). True love is always coming back to the cross —or never leaving it.

Day 4: Acts 2:37–47

Paul in Romans 5:5–6 says, 'God's love has been poured into our hearts through the Holy Spirit who has been given to us'. He immediately goes on to say what this love is: 'while we were still weak, at the right time Christ died for the ungodly'. Here what follows the coming of the Holy Spirit on the day of Pentecost is a very practical manifestation of the love of God—the full and free sharing and distribution of possessions and goods according to need, and the spending of time together in common meals and worship. Note that love is not engendered for its own sake, but it arises directly from the church applying itself to its core activities—the apostles' teaching, fellowship, the breaking of bread, and the prayers— by which the gospel of the crucified and risen Jesus is constantly asserted at the heart of the church's life. From this flow all the practical manifestations of love. (See also Acts 6:1–7, where, in the midst of practical love and caring, and the tensions that can arise within that, the apostles devote themselves even more purposefully 'to prayer and to the ministry of the word'—see v. 4.)

To think about: What is the fourfold core activity of the church, as set out in verse 42? How does the shared life of love flow from that? How does our own church's life compare with that at present?

Day 5: Acts 4:32 – 5:11

This shows us an extension of what happened in the previous passage. It also depicts how vital the Holy Spirit considers it in the life of the church, that we should be 'speaking the truth in love' (Ephesians 4:15). Were Ananias and Sapphira lost forever because of what they had done? We are not told. Presumably they were believers, and so would have arrived in glory very suddenly and with acute embarrassment. Certainly their concealment was a serious virus which, if allowed to remain in the church, could have infected the whole body and done severe damage. In this instance God obviously regarded the church in Jerusalem as being worth preserving, and better off without them.

To think about: 'Great fear came upon the whole church, and upon all who heard these things'. As well it might! But see what went on to happen in this cleansed and purified church, in Acts 5:12–16.

Day 6: 1 John 4:7 – 5:6

This is the classic passage on loving one another. It makes clear that love is from God, as manifested in the sending of His Son to be the propitiation for our sins. To receive the Spirit, confess Jesus as the Son of God sent from the Father as the saviour of the world, and so to love one another, is to abide in God and to have God abiding in us. When we say 'God is love', we are not answering the question, 'Who is God?' but the question, 'What is love?' God and His action defines what love is, and brings us in to it. Through the forgiveness of the cross we are freed from the fear of judgment and punishment, into the wholesome love of God and one another. The two are together as one. Loving God as He really is, and not loving one another, is impossible.

Question: Is there another person whom I do not love? Do I really know the love of God?

For Group Discussion:
'Forgiving one another, <u>as God in Christ has forgiven you</u> . . . live in love, <u>as Christ loved us and gave himself up for us</u>' (Ephesians 4:32; 5:2). What does it mean to say, 'Love is living towards others in the forgiveness of God' (Day 3)? How does this work out in practice?

'Those who do not love a brother or sister whom they have seen, cannot love God whom they have not seen' (1 John 4:20, Day 6). Why and how is this so?

Have you ever been in a situation where you love two other people who are not in love with each other? What was that like? 'Everyone who loves the parent loves the child' (1 John 5:2). Why does God <u>require</u> of us that we love one another if we are to belong in love to Him? What does that tell us about His association with each one of us? Is it possible to love God while being out of love with any other person?

'Eager to maintain the unity of the Spirit in the bond of peace' (Ephesians 4:3, Day 1). Note that Paul does not tell us to <u>make</u> this unity, but to <u>maintain</u> it as something already given by God and present in our midst. In what ways do we seek to make or set up unity or fellowship in the church? How is this different from what Paul says here? How do we discover and maintain the 'unity of the Spirit'?

Prayer: *Psalm 133.*

Week 32

BAPTISM

Day 1: Romans 6:3–11

Jesus said of his death on the cross, 'I, when I am lifted up from the earth, will draw all people to myself' (see John 12:31–33). On the cross he identified himself in love with all of sinful humankind. He was one with us. In baptism he gave us a practical way of being identified with him. Paul says in Colossians 2:12, 'You were buried with him in baptism, in which you were also raised with him through faith in the working of God, who raised him from the dead'. *Baptism is our identification with Jesus Christ in his death, burial and rising to life again.* 'As many of you as were baptised into Christ', says Paul, 'have put on Christ' (Galatians 3:27).

The baptised person is made one with the crucified and risen Jesus.

To think about: A Christian man was invited by friends to watch a 'blue movie'. 'I can't go in there', he said, 'I'm baptised!'

Day 2: Acts 22:3–16

In the Nicene Creed we say, 'We acknowledge one baptism *for the forgiveness of sins*'. Baptism, in which water comes over us in the name of the Father and of the Son and of the Holy Spirit, is a sign over the outside of what happens to us inside when we believe in Jesus Christ (see e.g. Acts 8:36, 37, 38). What Jesus did on the cross and in the resurrection becomes effective for us and we receive the glorious 'washing away' of sins. Here Paul has met the risen Christ and experienced his burning light. Now Ananias says, 'Rise and be baptised, and wash away your sins, calling on his name' (v. 16). Because what Jesus did was sufficient to deal once and for all with all our sins—past, present and future—baptism needs to happen to each person only once.

To think about: Water is a primal element in human life. Without it we cannot live, without it we cannot be clean. It can also be dangerous—in it we can drown. How do these things come together in baptism in our relationship with Christ?

Note: While for some, who advocate total immersion, the amount of water used is important, and has significant symbolic value, the Greek word 'baptise' is also used in Luke 11:38 to refer to washing a part of the body only. The true focus of baptism is not the action of baptising, but the action of God in Christ.

Day 3: John 3:1–17

Jesus spoke to Nicodemus of the new birth to eternal life by the Spirit of God which comes through believing in Jesus as the Son of man lifted up on the cross like the serpent in the wilderness (see Numbers 21:4–9). The words 'born of water and the Spirit', in verse 5, refer to the cleansing action of the Spirit in the forgiveness of sins, to bring us to this new birth as children of God. The immediate context was the fact that John was 'preaching a baptism of repentance for the forgiveness of sins', and that Jesus' disciples were also baptising with water (see Luke 3:3; John 1:24–34; 3:22–4:3), and Jesus may be emphasising here the importance of repentance in the new birth. 'Water and the Spirit' has generally been taken in the church to have a baptismal reference (though some for polemical or other reasons have dissociated it from the act of baptising). Nothing that baptism signifies can happen apart from the action of the Spirit of God, bringing new birth from above by virtue of Christ's cross. An Anglican prayer book says: 'Baptism is the sign and seal of this new birth' (*An Australian Prayer Book,* p. 519).

Question: Have I been born again? (Examine yourself in the light of this whole passage.)

Day 4: Acts 2:37–42

Repentance (see Week 24) is an integral part of the baptism package. Here it is specified along with the forgiveness of sins and the gift of the Holy Spirit (v. 38). So also *faith* is indispensable. Jesus said, 'The one who believes and is baptised will be saved; but the one who does not believe will be condemned' (Mark 16:16). Here again it is faith in *Christ* that makes the difference, rather than the act of baptising. See also how baptism issues in participation in the life of the church (v. 42; see also 1 Corinthians 12:13). You cannot baptise yourself—it is always done *to* you by someone else. It is never a private or solitary event, but a communal action in Christ.

To think about: Do I see my baptism as somehow apart or distinct from my coming to God in repentance and faith, or all part of the same bundle?

Note: Does 'the promise is to you and to your children' (v. 39) refer to those who are children now, or to (adult) generations yet to come? We are not told.

Those who baptise infants do not see this as any different in kind from the baptism of adult believers. Faith and repentance are still present, expressed in this instance by the parents (and godparents) on behalf of a family member who is included in the new covenant of grace (as children were included in the old covenant by circumcision; see Genesis 17:9–14; and Deuteronomy 6:4–9; see also 1 Corinthians 7:14). Where and how does faith and turning to God begin? Esau and Jacob's destinies were set before they were born (see Genesis 25:21–23). John the Baptist was filled with the Holy Spirit even from his mother's womb (Luke 1:15).

The matters of election, new birth, faith and repentance are wonderful mysteries of God's grace, before which we should hold ourselves in awe.

Day 5: Matthew 28:16–20

'In the name of the Father and of the Son and of the Holy Spirit' is not some ritual formula or correct form of words. It is literally '*into* the name ...' Baptism signifies admission into the very life and action of the Trinity, as 'children of God, by faith' (Galatians 3:26–27). This is in keeping with John 14:15–24: 'We will come to them and make our home with them'. Note also again that it is a communal action: nations, not just individuals, are to be brought into the life of God.

Question: Do I know myself to be *in* the Father, the Son and Holy Spirit? Embraced by the Father with the arms of the Son and the Spirit!

Day 6: Isaiah 11:1–10

Baptism is not only into the life, but also into the *ministry*, of Christ as Messiah. Churches which practise 'confirmation' (prayer for strengthening by the Holy Spirit with the laying-on of hands), often use a prayer which incorporates verses 2–3 here (see e.g. *A Prayer Book for Australia*, p. 61). The context makes clear that as 'Christ-ians' or 'Messiah-ites' we are brought into participation in Christ's action of bringing his word of justification to the nations (v. 4), with a view to the kingdom of God that is coming in the new heavens and the new earth (vv. 6–10; see also Isaiah 66:22–23).

Question: Have I come to see my baptism, and my status as a baptised person, in its eternal dimensions? Does this show in my practice from day to day?

For Group Discussion:
Let members of the group share their varied experiences of baptism, and what it now means to them personally.

What does it mean to say, 'All of us who have been baptised into Christ Jesus were baptised into his death' (Romans 6:3, Day 1)? Why should this be necessary? What does it mean to say that in baptism, 'you were also raised with him through faith in the power of God, who raised him from the dead' (Colossians 2:12)? What follows from this in our lives?

Repentance and faith, as well as belonging with others in the church, are all part of the baptismal 'package' (see Day 4). What happens when any one of these elements is dissociated from the physical act of baptising?

Our participation in the ministry of Christ as 'Christ-ians' looks towards 'the new heavens and the new earth' (Isaiah 66:22, see Day 6). What difference would it make if this was the perspective of every baptism, and of every baptised person?

Prayer: *Psalm 46.*

Week 33

THE LORD'S SUPPER

Day 1: John 6:25–40

Over against our determination to live by ourselves and from ourselves (which we were never designed to do), Jesus speaks to us of the true life that comes from God, in dependence upon Him by faith.

The manna in the wilderness (see Exodus 16:11–36) was a sign of this true way of life from God. Jesus himself is now the gift from God through whom we come into this eternal life—even from death.

We are to relate with him as closely as we do with what we eat. While we rush around trying to do the works of God ourselves, the true work of God is to believe in the one whom God has sent (v. 29), and so to be in the flow of His strong saving action.

Pray: 'Grant us, therefore, gracious Lord, so to eat the flesh of your dear Son Jesus Christ, and to drink his blood, that we may evermore dwell in him, and he in us. Amen' (*A Prayer Book for Australia*, p. 125).

Day 2: John 6:41–69

Our relationship with Christ is not some ethereal, mystical, indwelling. It has to do with the hard facts of Jesus' earthly life (v. 42), and particularly his death on the cross, as a sacrifice for sin. It was when Jesus began to talk about his flesh and blood as separated entities (separated by violence done to his body), and our intimate relationship with him in that action of the cross, that his listeners were scandalised and took offence. 'This is a hard saying', they said, 'who can listen to it?' (v. 60). At this point, 'many drew back and no longer went about with him' (v. 66). The cross is indeed offensive to the religious, who think they can place God under some obligation, and nonsense to the intellectuals, who think they can sort it all out themselves (see 1 Corinthians 1:22–24). But it is only as we come to the Jesus of that cross and say, 'That was necessary for me: I was crucified there in him, and now I live by faith in him, as the child of God'—that is the only way we can come into life as it is really meant to be.

To think about: 'As often as you eat this bread and drink the cup, you proclaim the Lord's *death* until he comes' (1 Corinthians 11:26). The sacraments are a proclamation of and participation in that action of the cross. The sacraments are not of us, nor of the church. The sacraments are of God, and of the cross.

Day 3: Luke 22:14–20

The significance of this action of Christ is set by its context—immediately before his suffering and death—and by what it was looking towards: the kingdom of God. Jesus speaks of the separating out of his body and blood—violence that will be done to him in the action of the cross. He links this with the bread and wine and tells them to eat and drink, signifying their participation in this, his action on their behalf. He tells them to repeat this action 'in remembrance of me'. 'Remembrance' here is not a bare memorial of a past event or person, it is an actual and dynamic participation in one who is alive. 'How can we have a memorial of one who is still alive, still our life?' (P. T. Forsyth). This continuing action was central to the life of the early church (see Acts 2:42, 46; 20:7), and has been in the church ever since.

Their experience of the risen Christ was that 'he was known to them in the breaking of the bread' (Luke 24:35).

To think about: 'In the word preached the saints hear Christ's voice; in the sacrament they have his kiss' (Thomas Watson—one of the 'Puritans').

Day 4: 1 Corinthians 10:1–17

The sacraments are not magic charms. Those participating in them will still come under judgment if their hearts are not with God. Indeed, their very participation may intensify the judgments (see 1 Corinthians 11:29–30) and place them more directly in the line of fire. This was the case for the Israelites who went through the 'baptism' of the Red Sea and ate and drank 'supernatural' food and drink from God. How much more is it true for us 'upon whom the end of the ages has come' (v. 11)? Paul here warns against idolatry and syncretistic worship mixed in with the pure worship of God 'in spirit and truth' (John 4:24). In that he has some beautiful things to say about our participation in the body and blood of Christ, and our unity with one another, in the Lord's Supper (vv. 16–17).

To think about: Do I presume on the grace of God, or take it lightly?

Day 5: 1 Corinthians 11:17–34

What does it mean to 'discern the body' in the Lord's Supper (v. 29)? The context provides the answer. First it is to have regard for Christ's body that died on the cross for us and his blood that was poured out there, and our participation in that (v. 27; see 1 Corinthians 10:16). But also *we* 'are the body of Christ' (see 1 Corinthians 12:12, 27). So we are also to be highly mindful of one another as we come to the Lord's Supper. There can be no such thing as 'my private communion'. Paul here focuses on caring relationships with one another as the only true and proper expression of participation in the body of Christ. To disregard Christ crucified and alive, and to disregard one another in the Lord's Supper, has serious consequences.

To think about: 'When you are offering your gift at the altar, if you remember that your brother or sister has something against you, leave your gift there before the altar and go; first to be reconciled to your brother or sister, and then come and offer your gift' (Matthew 5:23–24). What difference would it make if this principle was invariably applied to our participation in the Lord's Supper?

Day 6: Isaiah 25:6–9

The messianic banquet at the end of time! This is what Jesus was setting his sights on when he said at the Last Supper, 'I will never again drink of the fruit of the vine until that day when I drink it new in the kingdom of God' (Mark 14:25). His death and resurrection are what has made this feast accessible to all who will come. This is where death is swallowed up, and the reproach of God's people removed. The Lord's Supper always looks back to the cross, and forward to the new creation. We proclaim the Lord's death—until he comes!

To think about: What is your favourite food and drink? Jesus considered this banquet worth forgoing all other food and, indeed, life itself. Ponder his parable in Luke 14:15–24. What things here and now hinder my participation in that promised banquet?

For Group Discussion:
Let group members share their varied experiences of participation in the Lord's Supper, and say what importance it has in their lives.

In what way is the Lord's Supper a proclamation of the Lord's death? Why should it be necessary for us to participate in the body and blood of Christ in this way? How is it an anticipation of his coming-again?

In the light of 1 Corinthians 10:16 and 12:27, what does it mean to be 'discerning the body' (11:29) in the Lord's Supper? What are the consequences of not doing this? (See 1 Corinthians 11:17–34, Day 5.) Why should this be so?

'The sacraments are not of us, nor of the church. The sacraments are of God, and of the cross' (Day 2). What happens to the sacraments when they come to be seen primarily as actions of us, or of the church, detached from the action of God in the cross?

Prayer: *Psalm 116.*

Week 34

MINISTRY IN THE CHURCH

Day 1: Ephesians 5:21–33

This passage has implications for relationships between husbands and wives in marriage today, and also for the distinct and mutual ministries of men and women in the home and in the church today. But in the present context we should focus particularly on the relationship between Christ and his people the church. Paul says this is what the institution of marriage is really designed to reflect and participate in (vv. 31–32). Here Christ is the head or ruler over the church (v. 23), and the one who saves it. Christ put the church before himself (this *serving* is the true nature of ruling or headship, see Mark 10:42–45; 2 Samuel 23:1–4), when he 'loved the church and gave himself up for her' (v. 25). This was with a view to cleansing the church, to present us 'holy and without blemish' (vv. 26–27). This is Christ's present ministry with us now. He loves us as he loves his very self, and nourishes and cherishes us (vv. 28–30). We on our part gladly submit to such ministry or service (vv. 24, 33). These relationships in ministry reflect the relationship between Father and Son. Jesus said, 'The Father is greater than I', and, 'I and the Father are one' (John 14:28; 10:30). True subordination is the essence of true unity in the action of love. 'He was not inferior to God, but he was subordinate . . . Subordination is not inferiority, and it *is* godlike' (P. T. Forsyth, *God the Holy Father*, NCPI, Blackwood, 1987, p. 42. The whole passage is worth reading). There can be no true love outside rightly ordered relationships ('hierarchy'). This is not a popular notion today.

To think about: Matters of 'headship' and 'submission' are often caricatured and lampooned, or dismissed out of hand. In the Scriptures they are real, subtly-nuanced, mutual, tender and strong. Christ is totally identified with us in love, and takes full responsibility for us as our head. When have we experienced good leadership? What has been our experience of an absence of leadership, or when leadership has been poorly exercised, or contested?

Day 2: Ephesians 4:7–16

All ministry in the church is Christ's own, by virtue of his headship over all things for the church (see Ephesians 1:22). He gives to others to share in this ministry in different ways. 'Apostles' were the founding leaders of the churches. It may also include those engaged today in 'church planting' (as in 1 Corinthians 3:6). 'Prophets' speak the word of God to His people, and 'evangelists' announce the good news of God's reign over all. 'Pastors and teachers' may refer to the one function in the church—the two certainly go together (see Mark 6:34). The role of all of these gifted ministries is 'to equip the saints (i.e. all of God's people) for the work of ministry' that each one of us has. The goal of all ministry is maturity in Christ (vv. 13–16; compare Colossians 1:28).

To think about: 'The aim of our charge is love that issues from a pure heart and a good conscience and sincere faith' (1 Timothy 1:5).

Day 3: 1 Timothy 3:1–7

The 'Pastoral Epistles' to Timothy and Titus were written later, when ministry and leadership in the church had been developed according to certain patterns. We must be careful, however, not to read back our present understanding of terms like 'bishop' and 'deacon' into those early days. Nevertheless, it is the intention of, for example, the Anglican ordinal that our ministries today should be patterned on the biblical ministries, so these remain determinative for us today.

There were a number of 'elders' (Greek: *presbyter,* from which we get our word 'priest') in each church, who may have been simply the older and wiser members (see Titus 2:1–6). But there were elders who *ruled* over the church through labouring in *preaching and teaching,* who were to be especially honoured and remunerated in the church (see 1 Timothy 5:17–19; 1 Thessalonians 5:12–13; hence the title 'reverend'—'to be revered'!). It could be that these were called 'overseers' (Greek: *episcopoi,* from which we get the word 'bishop'). It is likely that there were a number of these in each local church (see Philippians 1:1). The designations 'overseer' and 'elder' appear to be interchangeable (see Titus 1:5–9; Acts 20:17, 28), and may be equivalent to the 'pastors and teachers' of Ephesians 4:11 (see also Acts 14:23; 1 Peter 5:1–5). The necessary qualities of such an 'overseer' are listed in this passage from 1 Timothy 3:1–7.

To think about: How are these biblical patterns of ministry different from what we have today? How are they the same? What differences would it make if the biblical principles of ministry were consistently applied today?

Day 4: 1 Timothy 3:8–13

1 Peter 4:10–11 makes the distinction between 'speaking' and 'serving' ministries, and says that both must come directly from God. 'Deacon' means simply a 'serving person', with responsibility perhaps for practical aspects of ministry. The seven in Acts 6:1–7 are not called 'deacons' but are given such a serving role. Note, however, that they, like those who have leadership in speaking the word of God, must also be wise and mature Christians, and some of them also engage in speaking ministries (Acts 6:8 – 7:60; 8:4–40). Women are included in the designation of 'deacon', such as Phoebe (Romans 16:1) who may well have been a rich benefactress of the church. Later in church history, deacons became responsible for the administration of poor relief (e.g. Lawrence in Rome, martyred AD 258) and of finance and property (hence 'arch-deacon'—a chief or ruling deacon).

To think about: What special areas of service need attention in the life of our church today? Who are our (official or unofficial) deacons?

Day 5: 1 Corinthians 14:26–40

In the early church, with its leaders in ministry, there was no such thing as a 'one-man band'—one minister who did everything. Corporate ministry was the rule, under right order and authority, by the Spirit, under God and Christ. That principle still holds today.

Verse 34 does not enjoin total silence upon women in the church gathering—see 1 Corinthians 14:5, 'I want you *all* to speak in tongues . . . prophesy' (compare Acts 21:8–9). First Corinthians 11:2–16 makes it clear that a woman is to pray or prophesy under the loving, caring, protecting authority of her husband and/or the church elder (the veil at that time was a cultural symbol of this authority, and of the freedom it gave to the woman—see 1 Corinthians 11:10, *RSV* note). This was not because of some anti-woman bias in Paul—note the number of women in ministry that Paul related to warmly and closely in Romans 16:1–16—but part of the way God has made men and women to be equal and mutually complementary, with distinct functions, in the unity of God's love-action (see also 1 Timothy 2:8–15). It is interesting that a similar silence regarding leadership in speaking the word of God is enjoined upon women in the home as well as the church (1 Peter 3:1–8), since this is given to the men (see e.g. Ephesians 6:4). Peter, in 1 Peter 3:4, sets out clearly the nature and strength of the woman's true ministry as an inner thing of the heart.

To pray about: To what ministry am I called in the church, or towards those outside?

Day 6: Romans 12:1–8

The purpose of any specific ministry within the church is to equip all God's people for the work of ministry, that their service/worship (same word in the Bible languages) may be pleasing and acceptable to God.

To think about: Are there any gifts of service that ring bells for me in verses 6–8?

For Group Discussion:

Think first of Christ's ministry towards his church, as in Ephesians 5:23, 25–30 (see Day 1). Let each member of the group spend some time in quiet to ask: How have I received this ministry of Christ? Then speak together of how we as the church receive that ministry of Christ to his bride.

Look at the distinction in 1 Peter 4:10–11 between 'speaking' and 'serving' ministries (see Day 4). What specific examples of these ministries do we see operating through the church today? Why are they necessary?

What is the place of headship and subordination in the ministry of the church today (see Day 1 and Day 3)? In what spirit and manner are these to be exercised? What happens when they are not present?

What are to be the qualities of an 'elder' or 'overseer' in the church (see Day 3)? Why are these particular qualities chosen, and how do they relate to Christ's own ministry in his church?

What are to be the qualities of a 'deacon', and why should this be so? How does this relate with Christ's own ministry in the world?

Look at the range of ministries operating in Romans 12:6–8 and 1 Corinthians 14:26–40. Which of these are present among members of the group? How can we encourage the better exercising of these ministries?

Prayer: *Acts 4:24–30.*

Week 35

THE WORK OF THE GOSPEL

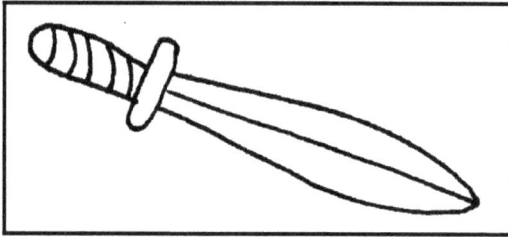

Day 1: Revelation 19:11–16

Jesus is the one who in this present age is bringing all things under the power and rule of the Father's love (see 1 Corinthians 15:20–28; Philippians 2:9–11), as the Father Himself places them subject to him. This happens purely and simply by the power of his word—he has no other weapon. Jesus is 'the Word of God', and he speaks the word of God to the whole world. This is the 'sword' that comes out of his mouth (see Ephesians 6:17; Hebrews 4:12–13). But note that he is not alone: 'the armies of heaven' follow him. These are all who in him bring his message to the nations.

Questions: Are we engaged with Christ in the bringing of his word to all nations (ethnic groupings)? Are we tempted to use any weapon other than his word?

Day 2: Isaiah 52:7–10

What is the message of the gospel ('good news' or 'welcome announcement')? Put most simply it is, 'Your God reigns' (v. 7). It is not just an invitation; it is a declaration of what is. By what happened on the cross and in the resurrection of Christ, the rule or kingdom of God has been incontrovertibly established forever at the heart of the universe. Paul says in 1 Corinthians 1:18, 'The message about the cross is foolishness to those who are perishing, but to us who are being saved it is the power of God'. So he says in Romans 1:16: 'I am not ashamed of the gospel; it is the power of God for salvation to everyone who has faith'. God, in His love and His victory over evil, rules supreme. It is for us to proclaim that this is so, and see men, women and children come under His sway. 'The feeble gospel preaches "God is ready to forgive"; the mighty gospel preaches "God has redeemed"' (P. T. Forsyth, *The Cruciality of the Cross*, p. 52).

To think about: Am I convinced that God rules over all? Am I happy for that to be so? How do I communicate that to others?

Day 3: Luke 24:25–27, 44–49

In both these resurrection appearances, Jesus refers to the scriptures of the Old Testament, and links them with his own death and resurrection. Then he tells the disciples that they are to go out and proclaim to the nations the 'repentance and forgiveness of sins' that has come in these things, by the power of the Holy Spirit. We are told that over these forty days before he ascended into heaven, Jesus spoke to them 'of the kingdom of God'. This then became the message of the apostles and others. The task of the apostles was to tell the events of Christ in the light of the Old Testament revelation, and to speak of the Old Testament in the light of the events of Christ. This they faithfully did, and their witness is recorded the New Testament. This record is now the substance of our apostolic gospel.

To think about: 'The Old Testament is not contrary to the New: for both in the Old and New Testament everlasting life is offered to Mankind by Christ' ('Articles of Religion', no. VII, in *An Australian Prayer Book,* p. 628).

Day 4: Acts 4:23–31

The early Christians' response to opposition and persecution was to pray for boldness to speak the word of God, and for Christ himself to confirm the word by the signs that accompany it (see Mark 16:15–20). That this prayer was answered immediately can be seen in what follows in Acts 4 and 5. Again in Acts 6, the apostles sense the need to ensure that prayer and the word of God are central to the church's life and ministry (Acts 6:4). As a result of their giving priority to these in their own ministry, we are told, 'the word of God increased' (Acts 6:7).

To think about: How do we meet resistance to the gospel? With silence, or with prayer for increased boldness to speak God's word?

Day 5: Acts 20:17–38

In this farewell message to the leaders of the church in Ephesus, Paul speaks of his activity among them. The many terms he uses to describe this are instructive: 'serving the Lord' (v. 19), 'declaring to you anything that was profitable' (v. 20), 'testifying . . . of repentance to God and of faith in our Lord Jesus Christ' (v. 21), 'to testify to the gospel of the grace of God' (v. 24), 'preaching the kingdom' (v. 25), 'declaring to you the whole counsel of God' (v. 27), 'to admonish every one with tears' (v. 31), 'the word of his grace, which is able to build you up and to give you the inheritance among all those who are sanctified' (v. 32). How Paul went about that in Ephesus is set out in Acts 19:1–20—note the time and commitment involved.

Question: Is that what we are doing?

Day 6: Romans 10:5–18

The word of salvation has been given to us, and we are to speak it, sent by God, if others are to hear and respond by faith. Meanwhile, God is making Himself known throughout all the world, so that all may be accountable to God.

Question: 'But how are they to call on one in whom they have not believed? And how are they to believe in one of whom they have never heard? And how are they to hear without someone to proclaim him? And how are they to proclaim him unless they are sent?' (vv. 14–15).

For Group Discussion:

Let members of the group tell of times when they have shared their faith with others, and times when they have not done so. Take care not to see this as some obligation imposed upon Christians, who should feel guilty if they fail to comply—or as some great merit badge if they have fulfilled the obligation! Let it be the coming out of what is inside: what has been called 'the overspill of the gospel from a heart too full to contain it'!

Ponder the picture of the rider on the white horse in Revelation 19:11–16 (see Day 1), with his one weapon of the word of God, as in Ephesians 6:17 and Hebrews 4:12–13. What difference does it make for us to know that it is <u>his</u> word and action when we come with the gospel?

The gospel 'is not just an invitation, it is a declaration of what is' (Day 2). When have you heard the gospel presented as an invitation? When has it come to you as a command? What is the difference?

'I personally believe that teaching is the best form of evangelism. I am not convinced that extremely simple pre-sentations of a few points with strong pressure to "make decisions" is the best way [to] bring life to the churches and the churches to life. Even so, I believe God uses all kinds of human endeavours, often in spite of ourselves, our ideas and our methods' (Geoffrey Bingham in Eager to Preach, *NCPI, Blackwood, 1998, p. 13). Paul the apostle took five hours a day for over two years to give 'the whole counsel of God' in Ephesus (see Day 5). Some modern-day 'evangelists' seek to bring people to Christ in minutes. Let members of the group each say briefly how they came to faith. What does that teach us about how the gospel is to be presented?*

Prayer: *Psalm 22:22–31.*

Week 36

THE LIFE EVERLASTING

Day 1: 1 Thessalonians 4:13–18

Death is not 'a natural part of life'. Death has come into the world as a consequence of sin (see Romans 5:12; Genesis 2:17; 3:19). It is an enemy to be destroyed (1 Corinthians 15:26). But to those who believe in Christ, death comes as an already defeated enemy. Christ has died, and Christ has risen, never to be subject to death again (Romans 6:9). His resurrection prefigures our own (Romans 6:5; 1 Corinthians 15:20–23). Such will be the wonder of this event, so far beyond anything that we have ever seen or heard or could imagine (1 Corinthians 2:9), that we must resort to picture language to speak of it, as in this passage. Rising from death and being together with the Lord forever is the reality being described.

To think about: Do I find these words comforting (strengthening) or alarming? Am I living my life now with a view to the resurrection to come, or have I tried to make some other compromise with death?

Day 2: John 5:19–29

Christ by his mighty saving death and resurrection has removed the sting of death, namely, the guilt of sin and the fear of judgment (see 1 Corinthians 15:54–57; Hebrews 2:14–15; 9:27). So he is able to say here that those who receive his word, and believe in the Father as the One who sent him, have eternal life already, and have already passed from death to life. As far as they are concerned, their judgment has already taken place in him on the cross (v. 24). Indeed, Jesus is able to say, 'I am the resurrection and the life. Those who believe in me, even though they die, will live, and everyone who lives and believes in me will never die' (John 11:25–26). He also said, 'Whoever keeps my word will never see death' (John 8:51). Others will see what they call our death, but we will not—we shall see the Lord (see Philippians 1:21–23).

The gift of life and of resurrection life comes from the Father, who has entrusted this action to the Son (vv. 21, 26). All judgment now is also focussed through the Son (vv. 22–23, 27; see Daniel 7:9–14). We are judged according to our response to the one whom God has sent (see Mark 8:38).

To think about: Have I already been through the judgment with Jesus in his cross? Am I now already in eternal life?

Have I acknowledged Jesus in my life, and am I acknowledged by him? Where do I stand now with regard to the fear of death?

Day 3: 2 Thessalonians 1:3–12

The coming of Christ at the end of the age will be a two-edged sword. It will show up how things really are. It will show where we stand in regard to Christ and what has been done for us in him. The gospel command has gone out: to repent and believe, to be forgiven and come to God as Father (see Acts 17:26–31). Those 'who do not obey the gospel of our Lord Jesus' and so 'do not know God' (v. 8) will by that final judgment be locked into their sin and their self-imposed 'exclusion from the presence of the Lord and from the glory of his might', which is the 'eternal destruction' of hell. 'To turn aside from thee is hell, To walk with thee is heaven' (J. G. Whittier, 'Immortal Love', *English Hymnal*, Oxford University Press, London, 1933, no. 408). On the other hand, 'all who have believed' will be in amazement and wonder to see the Lord Jesus and all he has done revealed in them in all his glory (v. 10, like the action replay or the sporting highlights with all the bad and boring bits chopped out!). Hence Paul's prayer in verses 11 and 12.

To think about: 'Nothing unclean will enter it, nor anyone who practises abomination or falsehood, but only those who are written . . . from the foundation of the world in the book of life of the Lamb that was slaughtered' (Revelation 21:27; 13:8). Jesus said, 'Rejoice that your names are written in heaven' (Luke 10:20).

Day 4: 1 Corinthians 3:10–17

There are two judgments that can be distinguished from each other at the end time. There is the judgment of salvation or condemnation, heaven or hell, eternal life or everlasting destruction. This, we have seen, is determined by where we stand with regard to Christ and his work for us. There is also the judgment of works—of rewards and losses according to what we have done. See Revelation 20:11–15: there is 'the book of life', which determines whether or not we end up in the 'lake of fire' (vv. 12, 15) and 'the books' by which we are judged according to what we have or have not done. These two judgments should not be confused. Here Paul is talking to believers in Christ—those who are building on the only sure foundation 'which is Jesus Christ'. So their position in heaven is assured (v. 15). But it is another question as to whether they will have anything to show for their lives that is of lasting and eternal value. Some of us may arrive there rather naked and empty-handed. The works that follow us into the kingdom will be the works of love wrought in us by the Holy Spirit through faith in Christ—the works of the Father's grace. There these will shine like jewels and precious stones (vv. 12–14, see Revelation 14:13; 19:8). Paul was determined to make a rich and full entrance into the eternal kingdom of our Lord and Saviour Jesus Christ, taking plenty in with him (see 2 Timothy 4:6–8; 1 Thessalonians 2:19–20; Colossians 1:24–29; 1 Corinthians 9:19–27; Philippians 3:7–21). We can be the same (see 2 Peter 1:3–11).

To think about: 'For this I toil, striving with all the energy which he mightily inspires within me' (Colossians 1:28–29).

Day 5: 1 Corinthians 15:35–58

The resurrection life and body are so far beyond anything that we know here in this life that words cannot describe them. Nevertheless, we have indications in the present creation that can help us understand. We are aware of different orders of being in the present creation, and of transformations that occur from one order to another (vv. 35–41). Our resurrection body will be as different from our present body as a plant is from the seed from which it grows—and as continuous with it (see also 2 Corinthians 5:1–5). A 'spiritual body' is not one that is less real than the physical body, but is this body glorified and eternalised in order to sustain the 'eternal weight of glory beyond all comparison' (2 Corinthians 4:17) that is coming to us (see vv. 42–50). Jesus' own resurrection body was the same body as before, yet changed (see e.g. Luke 24:36–43): a 'spiritual body', substantial and real, yet no longer subject to physical limitations, but moving in the freedom of his spirit, and able to come and go as he pleased.

To think about: What difference will there be when death is no longer present or powerful!

Day 6: Luke 19:11–27

The two judgments (see Day 4) are clearly set out in this parable of Jesus. There are those who have hated the king and rejected his rule, who receive their doom (vv. 14, 27). But the focus here is upon the servants of the king, and their judgment of rewards and losses on account of what they have done with the gifts from the king. Note the magnitude of the reward in comparison with the little gift (vv. 16–19)—whole cities to be in charge of in place of single pounds! Such will be the order of our privileges and responsibilities in the new creation. Other references too (e.g. Matthew 19:28–29; Luke 20:27–40; 2 Peter 3:13; Revelation 7:9–17; 21:1 – 22:5) indicate that this is when the fun will really begin!

To think about: 'The Spirit and the Bride say, "Come." And let everyone who hears say, "Come." And let everyone who is thirsty come, let everyone who desires take the water of life without price . . . The one who testifies to these things says, "Surely I am coming soon." Amen. Come, Lord Jesus! The grace of the Lord Jesus be with all the saints. Amen' (Revelation 22:17, 20–21).

For Group Discussion:

Let members of the group tell of experiences they have had in the death of another person, or when they have been close to death themselves.

'It is appointed for human beings to die once, and after that the judgment' (Hebrews 9:27). Death is the point of no return, when we are faced with our lives just as we have lived them. What part does fear of judgment play in our fears and evasions of the reality of death (see also Hebrews 2:14–15)?

What is the relationship between our death and Christ's death (see Day 2)? What difference does this make to our own approach to death?

What is the difference between the 'two judgments': the judgment of salvation/condemnation, on the basis of our faith in Christ, and the judgment of rewards/losses on the basis of our works (see Day 4 and Day 6)? Why are both important?

How is Paul's teaching on the resurrection of the body, based on God's action in Jesus Christ, different from the strongly prevailing notion (grounded in pagan Greek philosophy) of the automatic immortality of the soul? What are you expecting in the life to come?

Prayer: *Psalm 73:21–28.*

QUESTIONS FOR

WRITTEN ASSIGNMENTS

Some participants may find it helpful to focus more intently on the materials by doing written assignments. One or more questions could be chosen from each section.

Weeks 1–9

1. 'The primary thing in all history is creation' (G. C. Bingham). Comment on this in a survey of biblical material on God as the Creator and Provider of all, and God's purpose and goal in creating. (Weeks 1 and 2)

2. 'The commandments are the outshining of God's own nature . . . they set forth for us the functional operations of the universe . . . They are life lived in the direct presence and power of God' (Week 3).
   Examine the Ten Commandments and show how they are a revelation of God in His relationship with us. (Weeks 3–5)

3. Examine the passages Genesis 2–3, Isaiah 14:12–15, Ezekiel 28:11–19, and Romans 3:9–18 to delineate the issues involved in the Fall of humankind. (Week 6)

4. Why do people worship idols? What forms do idols take? What is the dynamic of idolatry? (Week 7)

5. What is the action of God's wrath in individual lives, and throughout history? Why is God's wrath not a popular theme, and how do we seek to evade it? (Week 8)

6. What covenants has God made with people? What is the importance of covenant in the Old and New Testaments? (Week 9)

Weeks 10–18

7. 'He was in the beginning with God' (John 1:2). Why do the apostles and others say that the one who came as Jesus pre-existed from the beginning? Who is this one? Why is it important for us to know? (Week 10)

8. 'And beginning with Moses and all the prophets, he interpreted to them in all the scriptures the things concerning himself' (see Luke 24:26–27, also Luke 24:44–49). How is the mission and ministry of Christ prefigured and prophesied in the Old Testament? (Week 11: feel free to range more widely through the Scriptures, or take a specific instance and examine it in depth.)

9. 'To you is born this day in the city of David a Saviour, who is Christ the Lord' (Luke 2:11). What is the importance of the birth and incarnation of Christ in the whole plan of God? Why was it necessary? (Week 12)

10. 'We have beheld his glory, glory as of the only Son of the Father, full of grace and truth' (John 1:14). What is the relationship between the Father and the Son, and how is this shown in the life and teaching of Jesus? What are the implications of this for us? (Week 13)

11. What do the Gospel accounts tell us of the meaning of Christ's suffering and death on the cross? How do the Epistles expand or add to this? What is the impact of that on our lives? (Weeks 14 and 15)

12. 'He preached Jesus and the resurrection' (Acts 17:18). What is the importance and significance for us of the apostolic testimony to the resurrection of Jesus? (Week 16)

13. Why did Jesus ascend into heaven? What is the purport of his present ministry—its source, dynamic, action, purpose and outcome? How do we see and experience its effects in our lives, or in our time? (Weeks 17 and 18)

14. What did Jesus himself teach about his coming again? How is this taken up in the Epistles and the Book of the Revelation? What is the pastoral importance of this teaching today? (Week 18)

Weeks 19–27

15. Who is the Holy Spirit? How is he related to the Father and the Son? (Week 19)

16. 'The Spirit searches everything, even the depths of God' (1 Corinthians 2:10). How does the Spirit communicate the depths of God to the depths of us? (Week 19)

17. Trace the work and promise of the Spirit in the Old Testament. (Week 20)

18. How is the Spirit related to the life and ministry of Jesus Christ? (Week 21)

19. Examine Jesus' teaching on the promised Spirit in John chapters 14 – 16. How was this fulfilled? (Week 22)

20. 'You shall receive power when the Holy Spirit has come upon you; and you shall be my witnesses in Jerusalem and in all Judea and Samaria and to the end of the earth' (Acts 1:8). Trace the work of the Spirit in the Acts of the Apostles. (Week 23)

21. 'The gifts of repentance and faith are the primary work of the Spirit.' Discuss. (Weeks 24 and 25)

22. 'The fruit of the Spirit is the law of God come into its own.' Discuss. (Week 26)

23. Why are the gifts of the Spirit needed, and how are they to be exercised? (Week 27)

Weeks 28–36

24. 'The reason God created us and everything that is was so He could have a wonderful family and a home for the

family to live in, and so set forth the glories of His true nature as Father.' Discuss. (Week 28)

25. What is the nature and purpose of God's selectivity with regard to His people in the way He operates in history? (Week 29)

26. Examine the terms 'Son of man', 'true vine', 'one new man', 'body of Christ' and 'the good shepherd' to describe the relationship of Christ with his people. (Week 30)

27. How do belonging to God and loving one another go together? (Week 31)

28. What is the place of baptism in our relationship with God? (Week 32)

29. 'You proclaim the Lord's death until he comes.' How does the Lord's Supper relate to these realities? (Week 33)

30. What is the nature and importance of headship in Christian ministry? (Week 34)

31. 'How are they to hear without a proclaimer?' Examine the place and power of the word of God in the ministry of the gospel. (Week 35)

32. What is the Christian hope with regard to death? (Week 36)

FOR FURTHER READING

This gives a list of further resources, mostly published by New Creation Publications, by which each topic may be followed through in more detail.

Week 1: Creator and Provider of All

Bingham, Geoffrey. *Mr Hicken's Pears*. Troubadour Press Inc., 1995.

———. *The Return of the Lorikeets*. Troubadour Press, Inc., 1995.

———. *The Lion on the Road*. Troubadour Press, 1994.

———. *For Pastors and the People*, section 1, 'The Doctrine of Creation'. NCPI, 1989.

———. *Creation & Reconciliation*. NCPI, 1987. (Also published as study 20 in *Living Faith Studies*, vol. 2. NCPI, 1981.)

———. *Can a Man Know God?* study 2 in Christian Teaching Series. NCPI, 1974.

———. *The Meaning and Significance of the Trinity*, study 3 in Christian Teaching Series. NCPI, 1974.

Kammermann, John. *Wild Men, Bread, and Pretty Stone*. NCPI, 1994.

Week 2: What Are We Made For?

Bingham, Geoffrey. *Comprehending the Kingdom of God.* NCPI, 2000.

——. *Everything in Beautiful Array.* NCPI, 1999.

——. *The Holy Spirit, Creation and Glory.* Redeemer Baptist Press, Castle Hill, 1999.

——. *Well Now . . . So Now You Are Truly You!* (leaflet). NCPI, 1998.

—— *Well Now . . . So You Are A Man!* (leaflet). NCPI, 1998.

——. *Man of Dust! Man of Glory!* NCPI, 1986.

——. *I, The Man!* NCPI, 1983.

——. *Bright Bird and Shining Sails.* NCPI, 1981.

——. *Salvation History.* NCPI, 1977.

——. *Oh, No, Lord! Not Law, Lord?!* NCPI, 1979.

Pennicook, Ian. *The Story of the Acts of God.* NCPI, 1994.

Week 3: What God Requires of Us

Bingham, Geoffrey. *Everything in Beautiful Array.* NCPI, 1999.

——. *Where I Love I Live.* NCPI, 1997.

——. *Ah, Strong, Strong Love!* NCPI, 1993.

——. *Liberating Love*. NCPI, 1988.

——. *The Splendour of Holiness*. NCPI, 1985.

Week 4: Our Duty towards God

Bingham, Geoffrey. *The Law of Eternal Delight*. NCPI, 2001.

——. *Sweeter Than Honey, More Precious Than Gold*. NCPI, 1995.

——. *The Way and Wonder of Worship*. NCPI, 1990.

—— *Dear Darling Idols: Lords and Gods Piffling and Appalling*. NCPI, 1981.

——. *Sabbath Rest or Human Turmoil?* NCPI, 1981.

——. *Oh, No, Lord! Not Law, Lord?!* NCPI, 1979.

Meatheringham, Deane. *The Delight of Law*. NCPI, 1977.

Week 5: Our Duty towards Our Neighbour

Bingham, Geoffrey. *The Profound Mystery: Marriage Love, Divine and Human*. NCPI, 1995.

——. *Love and Marriage*. NCPI, 1995.

——. *I Love the Father*. NCPI, 1990.

——. *God's Glory, Man's Sexuality*. NCPI, 1988.

——. *The Heavenly Vision*. NCPI, 1987.

——. *Man, Woman, and Sexuality*. NCPI, 1986.

——. *Angry Heart or Tranquil Mind?* NCPI, 1984.

——. *Oh, Father! Our Father!* NCPI, 1983.

——. *Truth—the Golden Girdle*. NCPI, 1983.

——. *The Sons of God Are the Servants of All*. NCPI, 1982.

——. *The God and Father of Us All*. NCPI, 1982.

——. *Father! My Father!* NCPI, 1977.

Week 6: God's Good Rule Rejected

Bingham, Geoffrey. *The Cleansing of the Memories*. NCPI, 1995.

——. *The Clash of the Kingdoms*. NCPI, 1989.

——. *If We Say We Have No Sin . . .* NCPI, 1987.

——. *The Conscience—Conquering or Conquered?* NCPI, 1987.

——. *I, the Man!* NCPI, 1983.

——. 'The Nature, Effects and Cure of Sin', study 24 in *Living Faith Studies*, vol. 3. NCPI, 1981.

——. *Freely Flows Forgiveness*. NCPI, 1981. (Also published as 'The Whole of Forgiveness', study 2 in *Living Faith Studies*, vol. 1. NCPI, 1981.)

——. *The Dominion of Darkness and the Victory of God*. NCPI, 1977.

——. *The Weakness of Man and the Power of God*, study 1 in Christian Teaching Series. NCPI, 1974.

Week 7: The Worship of Other 'Gods' (Idols)

Bingham, Geoffrey. *Dear Darling Idols: Lords and Gods Piffling and Appalling*. NCPI, 1981. (Also published as study 45 in *Living Faith Studies*, vol. 5. NCPI, 1981.)

Week 8: Wrath—The Pressure of God's Holy Love

Bingham, Geoffrey. 'The Vindication of God', study 33 in *Living Faith Studies*, vol. 4. NCPI, 1981.

Bleby, Martin. *The Vinedresser: An Anglican Meets Wrath and Grace*. NCPI, 1985.

Meatheringham, Deane. *The Judgements of God*. NCPI, 1983.

Week 9: God's Covenant Faithfulness

Bingham, Geoffrey. *The Magnificence of Mercy*. NCPI, 2000.

——. *Searching for God*. Redeemer Baptist Press, Castle Hill, 2000.

——. *Comprehending the Covenant*. NCPI, 1999.

——. *Love's Most Glorious Covenant*. Redeemer Baptist Press, Castle Hill, 1997.

Weeks 10 & 11: Who Is the Son?
What Is His Mission?

Bingham, Geoffrey. *Christ the Conquering King!* NCPI, 1985.

——. *The Person and Work of Christ*. NCPI, 1983.

——. 'The Person and Work of Christ', study 16 in *Living Faith Studies*, vol. 2. NCPI, 1981.

Weeks 12 & 13: Became One of Us
The Only Son of the Father

Forsyth, P. T. *God the Holy Father*. NCPI, 1987 (1897).

Weeks 14 & 15: Crucified, Dead and Buried
For Us and for Our Salvation

Bingham, Geoffrey. *Come! Let Us Go to Calvary!* NCPI, 1997.

——. *Christ's Cross over Man's Abyss*. NCPI, 1994.

——. *Beyond the Cross*. NCPI, 1988.

——. *The Word & the Words of the Cross*. NCPI, 1982.

Bleby, Martin. *The Vinedresser: An Anglican Meets Wrath and Grace*. NCPI, 1985.

Due, Noel. *The Holiness of God in P. T. Forsyth's Theology of the Atonement.* NCPI, 1986.

Forsyth, P. T. *The Cruciality of the Cross*. NCPI, 1994 (1909).

Weeks 16 & 17: He Rose Again
He Ascended into Heaven

Bingham, Geoffrey. *Comprehending the Resurrection*. NCPI, 2000.

——. *Christ the Conquering King!* NCPI, 1985.

——. *The Person and Work of Christ*. NCPI, 1983.

——. 'The Person and Work of Christ', study 16 in *Living Faith Studies*, vol. 2. NCPI, 1981.

Week 18: He Will Come Again

König, Adrio. *The Eclipse of Christ in Eschatology: Toward a Christ-Centred Approach*. NCPI, 1989.

Pennicook, Ian D. *Maranatha!* NCPI, 1998.

Weeks 19, 20, 21, 22 & 23:

Who is the Holy Spirit?

The Spirit in the Old Testament

The Spirit and Jesus

The Promise of the Spirit

The Coming of the Spirit

Bingham, Geoffrey. *Spirit-Baptism: Spirit-Living*. NCPI, 1990.

——. *The Person and Work of the Holy Spirit*. NCPI, 1985.

——. *The Day of the Spirit*. NCPI, 1985.

——. *The Christian and the Holy Spirit*, study 6 in Christian Teaching Series. NCPI, 1974.

Week 24 Repentance & Forgiveness of Sins

Bingham, Geoffrey. *Well Now . . . So You Are Forgiven!* (leaflet). NCPI, 1998.

——. *Well Now . . . So You've Changed Your Mind* (leaflet). NCPI, 1998.

——. *The Cleansing of the Memories*. NCPI, 1995.

——. *If We Say We Have No Sin . . .* NCPI, 1987.

——. *The Conscience—Conquering or Conquered?* NCPI, 1987.

——. *Freely Flows Forgiveness*. NCPI, 1981. (Also published as 'The Whole of Forgiveness', study 2 in *Living Faith Studies*, vol. 1. NCPI, 1981.)

——. 'The Principles and Practice of Evangelism', study 50 in *Living Faith Studies*, vol. 5. NCPI, 1981.

——. *Commanded Repentance and Full Forgiveness*, study 4 in Christian Teaching Series. NCPI, 1974.

Week 25: Faith and Belonging to God

Bingham, Geoffrey. 'The Nature and Meaning of Faith', study 4 in *Living Faith Studies*, vol. 1. NCPI, 1981.

——. *Faith Justification Conversion and the New Birth*, study 5 in Christian Teaching Series. NCPI, 1974.

Week 26: The Fruit of the Spirit

Bingham, Geoffrey. *Comprehending Fruitfulness to God*. NCPI, 2000.

——. *The Spirit's Harvest*. NCPI, 1987.

Week 27: The Gifts of the Spirit

Bingham, Geoffrey. 'The Giver: The Gifts: The Giving', study 3 in *Living Faith Studies*, vol. 1. NCPI, 1981.

Week 28: The Planned Family

Bingham, Geoffrey. *Comprehending the Family of God and Man*. NCPI, 1999.

——. *I Love the Father*. NCPI, 1990.

——. *Oh, Father! Our Father!* NCPI, 1983.

——. *The God and Father of Us All*. NCPI, 1982.

——. *Father! My Father!* NCPI, 1977.

Week 29: Called to God—Sent to Serve

Bingham, Geoffrey. *Christ's People in Today's World*. NCPI, 1985.

———. *The Church, Life, and Relationships*. NCPI, 1984.

———. 'Vocation: Calling and Election', study 38 in *Living Faith Studies*, vol. 4. NCPI, 1981. (Republished as *God's Calling: Our Response*. NCPI, 1993.)

Week 30: Christ and His Church

Bingham, Geoffrey. *Christ's Living Church—Today*. NCPI, 1993.

Bleby, Martin. *The Vinedresser: An Anglican Meets Wrath and Grace*. NCPI, 1985.

Week 31: Loving One Another

Bingham, Geoffrey. *Beyond Mortal Love*. Troubadour Press Inc., 1996.

———. *Where I Love I Live*. NCPI, 1997.

———. *Strong as the Sun*. Troubadour Press Inc., Blackwood, 1994.

———. *Twice-Conquering Love*. NCPI, 1993.

———. *Ah, Strong, Strong Love!* NCPI, 1993.

———. *Liberating Love*. NCPI, 1988.

——. 'The Nature and Meaning of Love', study 1 in *Living Faith Studies*, vol. 1. NCPI, 1981. (Republished as *Constraining Love*. NCPI, 1985.)

Bleby, Martin, 'The Gifts In and for Love—Forever', study 14 in *Giving and Thanksgiving in the Church*, Pastors' School 2000, Morning Sessions. NCPI, 2000.

Weeks 32 & 33: Baptism, The Lord's Supper

Bingham, Geoffrey. *The Things We Firmly Believe*, chapters 17 and 18 'The Church and the Sacraments'. NCPI, 1986.

Bleby, Martin. 'The Cross and the Sacraments' in *The Power and Preaching of the Cross*, Summer School, 1985. NCPI, 1985.

——. 'The Pastor and the Sacraments' in *Pastoral Proclamation and Worship in Today's World*, Pastors' School, 1986. NCPI, 1986.

——. 'The Word and the Sacraments' and 'The Ministry and the Sacraments', in *Crisis in Church and Kingdom*, Pastors' School, 1989. NCPI, 1989.

Bleby, Martin. *The Gift of God: Baptism and the Lord's Supper as Sacraments of the Cross,* NCPI, 2007.

Week 34: Ministry in the Church

Bingham, Geoffrey. 'Pastoral Dynamics Series', Monday Pastors' Study Group notes. NCPI, 2000.

——. *Primarily for Parsons*. NCPI, 1987.
——. *The Authority and Submission of Love*. NCPI, 1982.

'Eldership in the Scriptures', study 22 in *Living Faith Studies*, vol. 3. NCPI, 1981. (Republished as *Shepherds of the Flock: Eldership in the Scriptures*. NCPI, 1997.)

Forsyth, P. T. *God the Holy Father*. NCPI, 1987 (1897).

Week 35: The Work of the Gospel

Bingham, Geoffrey. *Christ's Message for Today's World*. NCPI, 1993.

——. *Proclaiming Christ's Gospel in Today's World*. NCPI, 1986.

——. 'The Principles and Practice of Evangelism', study 50 in *Living Faith Studies*, vol. 5. NCPI, 1981.

Meatheringham, Deane. *Your God Reigns: A Theological Foundation for Evangelization*. NCPI 1988.

——. *Gospel Incandescent*. NCPI, 1981.

Week 36: The Life Everlasting

Bingham, Geoffrey. 'Dear Friend or Dark Intruder? The Theology of Death', study 42 in *Living Faith Studies*, vol. 5. NCPI, 1981. (Republished as *Dear Death or Dark Devourer?* NCPI, 1994.)

——. *The Matter of the Millennium*. NCPI, 1991.

——. *The Revelation of St John the Divine: Commentary and Essays on the Book of the Revelation*. NCPI, 1993.

König, Adrio. *The Eclipse of Christ in Eschatology: Toward a Christ-Centred Approach.* NCPI, 1999.

Ian D. Pennicook. *Maranatha!* NCPI, 1998.

Many of these and other resources are available free on the New Creation Archive:

http://www.newcreationlibrary.net/index.html

God's Holy Love has been recorded as daily readings with comments (DR 1, 1998) for radio or private devotional use: 6 minutes a day, 6 days a week, for 36 weeks.

The series is also available in lecture form (BSWAC, 1994), and as lectures with some discussion (CTS 112, 2001).

Contact **Marble Media** for further information:

martin.bleby@gmail.com